TO

MY FATHER

WITH LOVE, WITH GRATITUDE

AND IN APOLOGY

WHO IS SYLVIA?

WHO IS SYLVIA?

A Light Comedy

BY

TERENCE RATTIGAN

HAMISH HAMILTON
LONDON

First published 1951
by HAMISH HAMILTON LTD
90 Great Russell Street, London, W.C.1

822
——
RAT

189214

PRINTED IN GREAT BRITAIN
BY WESTERN PRINTING SERVICES, LTD., BRISTOL

CHARACTERS
(*In order of appearance*)

MARK
WILLIAMS
DAPHNE
SIDNEY
ETHEL
OSCAR
BUBBLES
NORA
DENIS
WILBERFORCE
DORIS
CHLOE
CAROLINE

ACT I	1917 Summer. About 8.0 p.m.
ACT II	1929 Spring. About 6.30 p.m.
ACT III	1950 Winter. About 6.0 p.m.

The action passes in a flat in Knightsbridge

Who is Sylvia? was first produced at the Criterion Theatre, London, on October 24th, 1950, with the following cast:

MARK	...	...	...	...	*Robert Flemyng*
WILLIAMS	...	...	...	...	*Esmond Knight*
DAPHNE	...	...	...	...	*Diane Hart*
SIDNEY	...	...	...	...	*Alan Woolston*
ETHEL	...	...	...	...	*Diana Allen*
OSCAR	...	...	...	...	*Roland Culver*
BUBBLES	...	...	...	...	*Diana Hope*
NORA	...	...	...	...	*Diane Hart*
DENIS	...	...	...	...	*David Aylmer*
WILBERFORCE		...	...		*Roger Maxwell*
DORIS	...	...	...	...	*Diane Hart*
CHLOE	...	...	...	...	*Joan Benham*
CAROLINE	...	...	...	...	*Athene Seyler*

The play produced by ANTHONY QUAYLE
Settings and costumes by WILLIAM CHAPPELL

WHO IS SYLVIA?

ACT I

A first-floor flat in Knightsbridge. Large windows L. *look on to a quiet street. Door backstage leads into hall, and another* R. *into bedroom. The room has an air of bachelor distinction, the furniture being considerably better chosen and displayed than the furnishings which are rather drab and ordinary. Some good pictures, mainly Dutch landscapes. A bronze head of a girl, not too conspicuously placed.*

The time is about eight o'clock of a summer evening in 1917. *The light has begun to fade but, as the curtain rises, we can see the dining-table has been laid in the centre of the room, with two places. The room is empty.*

There is the sound of the front door closing and after a moment MARK *enters. He is thirty-two and plainly goes to a tailor in or near Savile Row. He is wearing a dinner jacket, single breasted, and a white waistcoat, and is carrying an object under his arm. This, as he removes the paper, is revealed to be a bottle of champagne. This he unwraps and places on the sideboard. Then he inspects the table, making a couple of meticulous changes. He next looks round the room, paying particular attention to the sofa whose cushions he rearranges. Then, on a sudden impulse, he goes to the window and pulls the heavy curtains, leaving the room in darkness for a moment, until he turns on the lights. These, after a second's consideration, he dims discreetly. Then he rearranges a small vase of flowers on the table. He stands back and examines the effect, but not entirely satisfied, sits in one of the chairs at the table. Mouthing soundlessly he makes animated conversation to the other chair,*

9

and we see that he has to lean his head to one side to circumvent the flowers. He therefore removes the vase.

Now, after a final glance round the room, he appears moderately satisfied. He takes a cigarette from a case, lights it and goes briskly to a telephone.

MARK (*into receiver*). Hullo . . . I want Sloane 7838, please. (*As he waits he still glances round the room.*) Cunliffe? . . . Yes . . . Is her Ladyship there? . . . Yes, please, . . . Hullo, darling . . . Darling, I'm afraid the most awful thing has just happened. A long dispatch from Mesopotamia has just this second come in, and it looks as if I won't be able to get home till very late. . . . Oh no, midnight, I should think, at the very earliest. It might be much later than that, even . . . Who? Oh, your father. Well, tell him how very sorry I am to miss him, will you? . . . Oh no, darling, don't bother to do that—I'll have a snack here in the office . . . Oh no, that's all right. One has to get used to these things in war-time . . . Mesopotamia . . . Well, it's the cypher they use, you see, one of the most complicated there is in the world . . . Yes. Kiss Denis for me—tell him to be good . . . Oh, did he? (*Submissively.*) Oh, yes, darling, I quite agree. Very naughty. Yes, darling, I'll talk to him in the morning . . . Oh yes, very severe, I promise . . . I'm so sorry about tonight . . . Goodnight. (*He rings off and jiggles the telephone for the Exchange.*) Hullo . . . Are you there? Yes, I've finished thank you. I want Victoria 8440 . . . Hullo, Foreign Office? This is Lord St Neots. Who's in charge of the Middle East department tonight? Well, it's a simple question, I should have thought you could have given me a reasonably simple answer . . . Look, dear lady, this is Lord St Neots. I work at the Foreign Office. I have worked at the Foreign Office for the past nine years. I simply want to know . . . Now how the dickens can I identify myself on the tele-

phone? I am Viscount St Neots, the son of the Earl of
Binfield. I am married. I have one child, a boy, aged five,
named Denis, and I live at No 58 Belgrave Square. Now,
dear lady, if there is anything else I can tell you about
myself I should be only too happy . . . (*Furiously.*) Well,
you can tell Mr Mole from me that he's a blithering
idiot. If I were a German spy I wouldn't go dashing
about ringing up the Foreign Office asking who's in
charge of the Middle East department. I'd jolly well
know who was in charge of the Middle East department.
Come to think of it, I'd probably *be* in charge of the
Middle East Department. (*He is rather pleased at this one,
and chuckles appreciatively.*) Very well, ring off, if you
wish. I have said my say. (*He jiggles the telephone again.*)
Hullo, Exchange? Get me Victoria 8440 again would
you. I got cut off . . . (*In an assumed voice most inexpertly
and suspiciously guttural.*) Hullo, Foreign Office. Please
might I with the Middle Eastern Department to speak!
Hullo, Middle East? (*In his normal voice.*) Who's in
charge there tonight? Mr Seymour? Good. Put me on
to him, would you . . . Charley? This is Mark—Do me a
little favour, would you? If my home rings up I'm with
you, deciphering a long dispatch about Mesopotamia,
and can't talk for fear of dropping a stitch. . . . What. . . .
That's better, isn't it? Gone out for a cup of coffee. You
obviously have experience . . . No. I have none,—
honestly I haven't. First time in seven years. Believe it
or not, it's true . . . No. Not ashamed of myself, yet.
Tomorrow, perhaps. Not now . . . Oh by the way,
Charley, if my home should ring you'd better have this
number, hadn't you. It's Sloane . . . Damn, I've forgotten
it. I know it so well, too. No, it's not on the receiver . . .
I tell you what. It's in the book under the name of Oscar
Philipson—got that? Oscar Philipson, and the address
is 12 Wilbraham Terrace, Knightsbridge . . . Yes, that's

right. Thank you, Charley, I hope I shall be able to do the same for you one day . . . (*As an afterthought.*) Oh, by the way, give my best to your wife.

WILLIAMS, *Oscar Philipson's manservant, enters. He is small, neat, rugged and (for he is an ex-batman) his "Sirs" and "My Lords" are military rather than domestic.*

WILLIAMS. Oh, you're here, my Lord.

MARK. Hullo, Williams.

WILLIAMS. I didn't know. I was just going out. I hope everything's all right?

MARK. (*rising*). Yes, thank you, Williams. Perfect, I think.

WILLIAMS. Of course. if you'd have let me know a bit earlier I could have made plans to stay in——

MARK. That's quite all right. As a matter of fact I'm very glad you're going out. I mean, it's kind enough of you to do what you have, anyway——

WILLIAMS. Oh, that's all right, my Lord. I was glad of the chance, to be honest. One gets a bit fed up with nothing to do all day—just sitting along there in the kitchen, waiting for the Captain's next leave——

MARK. Any news of him, Williams?

WILLIAMS. I had a line from him about a week ago—giving me notice as it happens—of course, joking, you know the Captain——

MARK. What had you done?

WILLIAMS. Well, in my last letter to him I said to him how I heard the war was going wonderfully and he'd be sure to be home for Christmas.

MARK. And Captain Philipson took umbrage, did he?

WILLIAMS. Well, out in France, as you know, things look a bit different to the way they do from here. I remember when I was on the Somme, just before I got my packet, I used to get proper fed up with letters from home, telling me how gloriously I was advancing when I'd been stuck in the same ruddy hole for three weeks.

MARK. I didn't know you were on the Somme—I just missed it.

WILLIAMS. Did you get a blighty?

MARK. No. I was only out there by kind permission of the Foreign Office; and last year they withdrew their kind permission—that's all.

WILLAIMS. I suppose you get white feathers?

MARK. Enough to stuff a pillow.

WILLIAMS. So do I. One old duck said to me yesterday on the tube—"Young man," she said, "why aren't you in uniform?" And I said, "Because there's a ruddy war on, you silly old sausage." Proper mad, she got. Called the conductor and all. (*He chuckles at the reminiscence.*) Well, my Lord, is there anything more I can do for you, because I ought to be getting along?

MARK. No, thank you, Williams. I'm very grateful.

WILLIAMS. Oh—do you see I put the lady out for you?

MARK. The lady?

WILLIAMS. The bust.

WILLIAMS *points to the bronze girl's head on the pedestal.*

MARK. Oh, yes.

WILLIAMS. The Captain had it in the lumber room. If you ask me he's never properly appreciated it. I think it's beautiful.

MARK. Thank you, Williams.

WILLIAMS. Must be wonderful to be able to do things like that.

MARK. Oh well, it's only a hobby, you know——

WILLIAMS. It ought to be more than a hobby, if you ask me. It ought to be an occupation. If I could sculpt or paint or something like that, I'd be at it all day long. Of course I've got my reading, but that isn't quite the same thing. (*Seeing the champagne.*) I see you brought the champagne. I know Captain Philipson would have been only too glad to have let you have one of his—

(*picking up champagne and putting it in ice bucket.*)

MARK. No. That would be stretching his hospitality too far. By the way, I've written to Captain Philipson telling him about tonight——

WILLIAMS. Yes, my Lord.

MARK. Oh, and Williams (*slightly embarrassed.*) Just supposing I—er—got caught in a sudden storm, or something—and—er—wanted to stay the night, would that be all right, do you think?

WILLIAMS. Yes, my Lord, of course. Only too easy. The bed is made up.

MARK. Of course, I probably won't be needing it at all——

WILLIAMS. You never know, my Lord. It's very hot to-night. I should say there's a good deal of thunder in the air. Just leave a note for me, would you, so I'll know.

MARK. Yes, I will. Oh, Williams—just in case I don't see you to thank you—(*He takes out his wallet.*)

WILLIAMS. No, my Lord, there's no need to do that.

MARK *gives him a pound.*

Oh, well—that's very kind of you, I'm sure.

MARK. Going out with your girl?

WILLIAMS. I haven't got a girl. Not steady, that is. I don't hold with it.

MARK. Don't hold with going steady?

WILLIAMS. No, my Lord. It's bad for a man's morale, getting tied up to one woman all his life—at least that's the way I see it. It eats into his soul—makes him old before his time.

MARK. Williams—you're speaking to a married man.

WILLIAMS. Oh well—*chacun à son goût,* as they say. Mind you, I'm not saying there's not a lot to be said for the blessed state—provided you don't let it get you down. But too many married men do, and there's the trouble.

MARK. I think there's something in what you say, Williams——

WILLIAMS. It's not so much me that says it, my Lord, as H. G. Wells. Very illuminating Wells.

There is a knock at the front door.

MARK. My God! That must be my guest.

WILLIAMS. Hope she hasn't been ringing long. You can never hear the bell from here. I'll let her in.

MARK. (*Distractedly*). No. I think perhaps you'd better let me do that, Williams, if you don't mind. You see, I haven't had time yet to explain to her about this flat—I merely gave her this address.

WILLIAMS. Oh. Doesn't she know who you are my Lord?

MARK. No. I haven't actually told her my name yet.

WILLIAMS. Well, what name have you told her?

MARK. Damn it, man, I haven't told her any name. We just don't happen yet to know each other awfully well, that's all. It takes such an infernally short time for a bus to get from Whitehall to Hyde Park Corner.

WILLIAMS. Ah. One of those. I see, my Lord. Well, I'll just slip along to the kitchen and when you've let her in I'll nip out.

MARK. Yes, do. (MARK *starts for hall, then turns back.*)

Another knock at the front door.

Williams! You think a name is advisable?

WILLIAMS. Oh. Very highly.

MARK. What do you suggest?

WILLIAMS. (*After considering*). The Captain uses Mason a lot.

MARK. I don't like Mason. Too rugged. What about Robinson?

WILLIAMS. You don't look a Robinson.

MARK. Smith?

WILLIAMS. No. That's fatal. (*After considering.*) Featherstonhaugh?

MARK. Don't be idiotic.

A third knock.

My God—she'll go in a second. I know—Wright.

How do you like that? Rather good, isn't it? Wright it shall be.

WILLIAMS. Yes, my Lord. I mean, very good, Mr Wright. *Bonne Chance.*

They disappear, MARK *in the lead. After a pause we hear the front door closing and voices in the hall.*

MARK. (*Off*) I hope you found it all right.

DAPHNE. (*Off*) Oh, yes. Quite easy really, only two stops in the tube from Notting Hill.

DAPHNE *enters, ushered in by* MARK. *She is in the early twenties and her face, partly concealed under a terrible hat—for she is not in evening dress—bears a marked resemblance to the bronze head. Her accent might be described as cautious.*

DAPHNE. Oh, look at you in evening dress. You are awful. You said not to——

MARK. Well—only a dinner jacket, you know. Doesn't really count.

She looks round the room.

DAPHNE. (*Rapturously*). Oh pictures! I love pictures, don't you? Of course, I can see you do. Oh, we've got one just like that at home (*She stands in front of a picture gazing at it with the eye of a connoisseur.*)

MARK. (*Behind her*). That one's by a Dutch painter.

DAPHNE. Oh, is it? (*She gazes at it.*) Of course, the colours are different in ours and there are more cows. It's called "Dawn on the Highlands". Who would that be by do you think?

MARK. Well—it could be by quite a lot of people.

DAPHNE. (*A shade scornfully*). I must ask Mr Fortescue. He'll know. Mr Fortescue's my boss at the office. He's wonderful really. He knows everything there is to know about everything.

MARK. He sounds wonderful.

DAPHNE. He is. (*In a confidential murmur.*) I say, old bean, where's the oojah?

MARK. The oojah?

DAPHNE. The om-tiddly-om-pom.

MARK *still looks baffled.*

The umpti-poo.

MARK. (*Light breaking*). Oh, the umpti-poo. How foolish of me. It's through this door here, and then on the right. (*He opens the bedroom door.*)

DAPHNE. (*As she passes him*). You didn't mind me asking, did you, old fruit? I do think a girl should be modernistic these days, don't you?

MARK. (*With enthusiasm*). I quite agree. As modernistic as she can possibly be.

DAPHNE *goes out.* MARK *goes to the sideboard and starts to undo the caviare. There is a discreet knock at the hall door.* WILLIAMS *then opens it.*

WILLIAMS. She's in there, isn't she?

MARK. That's right. The oojah.

WILLIAMS. I saw the light on. I brought this, some nice hot toast for the caviare. (*He comes to table with it.*)

MARK. Thank you very much, Williams.

WILLIAMS. I say, I got a squint at her coming in. Do you know, my Lord, who she's the living spittin' image of?

MARK. No. Who?

WILLIAMS. That girl there. (*He points at the bronze head.*)

MARK. Oh! Do you think so?

WILLIAMS. Not a doubt of it. In fact, I thought perhaps she'd sat to you for it. She didn't, did she?

MARK. No, Williams. No one sat to me for that.

WILLIAMS. From imagination, was it?

MARK. From memory.

WILLIAMS. Who of?

MARK. Of a girl I knew once.

WILLIAMS. Um, terrible hat. Never make the best of themselves, do they?

B

MARK. Very rarely. (*Nervously.*) Er—Williams—don't
you think——

WILLIAMS. That's all right, my Lord. She's still there. I
can see the light from here. As I was saying, it's wonderful what these girls do to themselves in the name of
beauty. Now the Captain's got a friend—his latest—
Ethel—have you met her, my Lord?

MARK. (*Distrait*). I don't know, Williams. So many of the
Captain's friends seem to be called Ethel.

WILLIAMS. You couldn't mistake *this* Ethel. What she puts
on herself you wouldn't hardly believe. Holy terror, she
is—least, not so holy, I suppose, but a terror all right.
I remember once—look out, my Lord. Lights are off.
Vive le sport.

*He disappears through the doors and closes them gently after
him.*

After a moment DAPHNE *comes through the bedroom door.*

MARK. Oh, hullo.

DAPHNE. Is that your garden, out there?

MARK. What? Oh yes. It belongs to this flat.

DAPHNE. Nice having a garden—especially this weather.

MARK. We might sit out there, later.

DAPHNE. Yes. That'd be nice. How do you get to it?

MARK. From the bedroom.

DAPHNE. Oh. (*After a faint pause.*) Yes. That'd be very
nice.

MARK. Look, shall we sit down? I'm afraid it's only cold,
you know. The fact is this is my man's night out.

DAPHNE. (*Seating herself*). Terrible the servant problem
these days, isn't it? It's all this bolshevism about.

MARK, *having seated her, helps her to caviare, with some cere-
mony.* DAPHNE *watches it going on the plate with bewilder-
ment, but is too polite to ask what it is.*

MARK. Yes. I expect so.

DAPHNE. (*Inspecting the caviare cautiously*). It's funny—

you wouldn't really expect the Russians to go and abdicate their Czar like that, after all these years, would you? On the other hand you've got to see two sides to every question, haven't you, and there's no doubt that he'd rather been asking for it, carrying on the way he has all this time, and Rasputin and all that. And then, of course, there's always social economics, isn't there, eh?

MARK. I'm so sorry. I didn't quite follow——

DAPHNE. I was giving my views on what's happened in Russia.

MARK. Oh, I see. Yes. I cordially agree. There's always social economics—(*He has been trying to open the champagne. He now succeeds.*) Ah. There we are. (*He pours some into her glass and into his own.*)

DAPHNE. Oo. Lovely! Sparkling gigglewasser.

MARK. I beg your pardon?

DAPHNE. It's a name for champagne. Giggle-water, you see, and then the German for water being wasser, it becomes gigglewasser.

MARK. But this isn't German champagne.

DAPHNE. I never said it was, silly. It's just a name Mr Fortescue invented for champagne—

MARK. Oh, I see. Mr Fortescue. (*He sits down opposite her.*) Er—this is Lanson '04. (DAPHNE *takes a sip.*)

DAPHNE. (*At length*). So it is. '04. Fancy. (MARK *looks at her but says nothing. He notices that she is not eating and divines the cause.*)

MARK. I do hope you like the caviare. If you don't, I can assure you that Messrs Fortnum and Mason will answer for it with their lives.

DAPHNE *lets out a merry peal of laughter.* MARK *looks pleased that his little joke has gone down so well.*

DAPHNE. You sounded just like Mr Fortescue when you said that.

The smile fades from MARK's *face.*

MARK. Oh? Did I?

DAPHNE. Shall I let you into a little secret? This is my very first taste of caviare.

MARK. Well, there has to be a first time for everything, doesn't there? Toast?

DAPHNE. Practically everything. (*Attacking some caviare with a spoon.*) Well, here goes. (*She takes a mouthful and patently finds it distasteful. But she recovers quickly.*) It's quite nice, really, isn't it?

MARK. I think so. (*He holds up his glass.*) Here's to a pair of the most beautiful eyes I've ever seen on any human being in all my life——

DAPHNE. Quite the Oscar Wilde, aren't you? (*She takes a sip and giggles.*)

MARK. (*Rises*). Look, I'm afraid you're not enjoying that caviare very much——

DAPHNE. Well, now you mention it, I never was much of a one for fishy things.

MARK. Then let's pass on to the next course. (*He removes the plates.*)

DAPHNE. Seems a pity, though—it's awfully expensive, isn't it?

MARK. Oh well. Expense is only a relative term, isn't it?

DAPHNE. Oh yes. Absolutely relative, isn't it? (*He places the next course before her.*) Oh, chicken. Now that *is* nice.

MARK. I'm glad we're on safer ground with chicken. (*He begins to pour her another glass of champagne.*)

DAPHNE. Oh, no. Stop. I don't want to get squiffy. You don't know how I carry on when I'm squiffy.

MARK. No, I don't. But I should very much like to.

DAPHNE. (*Looking up at him*). I might do things I might regret.

MARK. (*Seductively*). *You* might regret them. But would I?

DAPHNE. You've really quite a way with you, haven't you?
Oh, well—just up to there——

She indicates the spot on the glass to which MARK *is permitted to pour.*

Whoa! That's lovely. Well. (*Extending her glass.*)

Here's to living, here's to dying,
Here's to laughing, here's to crying,
Here's to this and here's to that,
But chiefly here's to that.

MARK. One of Mr Fortescue's?

DAPHNE. Yes. How did you guess?

He puts champagne in ice-bucket, then returns to table and resumes his seat.

MARK. I've no idea. (*He extends his glass.*) Now I'll give
you a toast. I'll just say—Here's to love——

DAPHNE *giggles. There is an appreciable pause while both get on with the business of eating.*

DAPHNE. You know, I don't know very much about you,
do I? I don't even know your name.

MARK. Don't you?

DAPHNE. What is it?

MARK. Mark.

DAPHNE. Mark? (*After a second's reflection.*) Yes, I like
that.

MARK. Do you? I'm so glad.

DAPHNE. (*Firmly*). It's a *nice* name, Mark. What's your
surname?

MARK, *in the act of taking a sip of wine, coughs. He takes rather more time to recover than seems necessary. From his expression of acute concentration it is fairly plain that he has forgotten his chosen pseudonym.*

MARK. (*At length*). Well, now—why don't you guess?

DAPHNE. Well, it could be almost anything, couldn't it?

MARK. Yes. Indeed it could.

DAPHNE. (*A shade scornfully*). It's not Smith, is it?

MARK. Oh no. It's definitely not Smith. I hate Smith.

DAPHNE. Yes, it is rather common, isn't it?

MARK. (*desperately*). I love *your* name. Now, Daphne Prentice is a charming name——

DAPHNE. Oh. I'm glad you think so. I always do think it's rather *nice*—though I say it who shouldn't.

MARK. Exquisite. It has music . . . I know—Wright!

DAPHNE. I beg your pardon?

MARK. (*Easily*). Wright. Mark Wright. That's my name. Do you like that?

DAPHNE. No.

MARK. (*With a slight laugh*). Oh, dear. Why not?

DAPHNE. I just don't think it's very nice, that's all.

MARK. (*A shade defiantly*). Well, what other name *would* you have thought nice?

He glances at the door.

> Featherstonhaugh?

DAPHNE. Oh, no. That's silly.

MARK. I cordially agree.

There is a pause.

DAPHNE. (*Meditatively*). Percy Pennyfeather's nice, don't you think?

MARK. Yes, I suppose it is. And so is Fortescue. But you know, Daphne, quite honestly, I don't think that either of them are really as nice as Wright. Just have another sip of champagne, and you'll see how nice Wright is. Go on.

She does so, and lowers her glass. MARK *instantly pours more champagne into it.*

DAPHNE. Oh, you are awful, aren't you?

MARK. There. Now, doesn't Wright sound better to you?

DAPHNE. Yes, it does, in a way. It rather grows on you, doesn't it? Mark Wright. Mark Wright. It's straightforward anyhow.

MARK. Simple and honest and direct, isn't it? No frills about it. Mark Wright. I must say I like it myself very much indeed. Mark Wright. (*He takes a sip of wine in silent toast to his new name.*)

DAPHNE. What do you do for a living?

MARK *puts his glass down carefully.*

MARK. Well, why don't you have another guess?

DAPHNE. I say, old bean, you do like guessing games, don't you?

MARK. After all, there aren't nearly so many occupations as there are names. (*An idea has struck him at the word "occupations".*) You really ought to be able to guess my occupation, Daphne.

DAPHNE *is reluctant to try.*

All right, I'll put you out of your misery. I'm a sculptor.

DAPHNE. A sculptor?

There is a pause while DAPHNE *wrinkles her brows in thought.*

MARK. (*Anxiously*). You think that's nice, don't you?

DAPHNE *still ponders for a moment.*

DAPHNE. (*At length*). Yes, I do. I think it's quite nice.

MARK. Splendid.

DAPHNE. What sort of things do you sculpture?

MARK. Well (*He rises and crosses to bronze head.*) That, for example.

DAPHNE. (*Turning her head*). That? (*She gazes at it in silence.*)

MARK. (*Anxiously again*). Nice, don't you think?

DAPHNE. (*Peering*). I can't see it properly.

MARK. I'll get it for you.

He brings the head over and places it on the table. DAPHNE *gazes at it.*

DAPHNE. Who is it?

MARK. Just a girl.

DAPHNE. Oh. No one special?

MARK. On the contrary. Someone very special. Don't you
think she looks like you?

DAPHNE. Well, I don't know that I feel altogether
flattered I must say.

MARK. (*A shade sharply*). Well, you should. If you don't
it's my fault. She was very beautiful.

DAPHNE. Was? Is she dead?

MARK. No. Only she probably doesn't look anything like
this now. This is how I remembered her as she was—
let me see now—I was seventeen then and I'm thirty-
two now—fifteen years ago—(*He is lost in reverie as he
gazes at the head.*)

DAPHNE. Go on. Tell me about her——

MARK. There's very little to tell, I'm afraid. You'd be
disappointed.

DAPHNE. Oh no. That's all right. I love a story.

MARK. Well, I was seventeen, as I told you. She was
sixteen. I met her—of all places—at a garden party.
The young people were forced to play tennis. Our
hostess made us partners, this girl and I—and we played
rather well together, although heaven knows I was
never any good at the damn game. We won: 6:3, 6:2.
After that we went for a walk together, not very far or
for very long, because we both knew our parents were
hating the party and would be wanting to go home
soon. At a certain spot where there was a stile and a
dead tree she let me kiss her—just once—and then we
went back to the party. On the way home we talked
about opera. I dropped her with her parents and that
was the last I ever saw of her. A month later I heard
she'd gone with her family to South Africa, and she's
been there ever since. She married a man called
Willoughby-Grant, and they live near Capetown. A
very pleasant house, somebody told me—right by the
sea.

He stops. DAPHNE *looks at him, bewildered.*

DAPHNE. Is that all the story?

MARK. Yes. That's all.

DAPHNE. Well, really, I must say. I see what you mean
about my being disappointed——

MARK. You like stories with more action?

DAPHNE. Well, I like them to have a happy ending, anyway.

MARK. (*Smiling at her*). Perhaps this one *has* a happy
ending.

There is a pause, broken by the ringing of the telephone.

Oh damn! (*He gets up.*) Excuse me. (*He goes to the
telephone. Into receiver.*) Hullo? . . . Yes . . . Right, thank
you, Charley. (*He rings off, then stands in doubt and
apprehension, looking at* DAPHNE.) Er—look; Daphne—
I wonder if I could ask you to do something.

DAPHNE. (*Ever cautious*). Rather depends what it is,
doesn't it?

MARK. Yes. But this isn't very difficult. Would you mind
awfully leaving me alone while I make this telephone
call? It's very confidential, you see.

DAPHNE. Confidential? Oh, well—that's quite all right.
(*She gets up.*) You give me suspicions, you know——

MARK. What suspicions?

DAPHNE. I'll tell you later. (*She goes into the bedroom.*)

MARK *lifts the receiver.*

MARK. Sloane 7838, please . . . (*He waits for the answer in
some evident trepidation, but when he speaks, his voice is
certainly solicitous.*) Hullo, darling. Did you ring me?
I was out having a cup of coffee and a bun . . . Oh,
plodding ahead, you know, plodding ahead. Who? . . .
Your father? . . . Oh, does he? All right . . . Oh, good
evening sir . . . What? Full moon? Yes, I think there
is . . . Why? . . . Zeppelins. Oh, no sir. The zeppelin
threat, I assure you, is now finally over . . . Cellar?

Oh, no sir. The boy is perfectly safe where he is unless there is an alarm . . . But he's not afraid of the zeppelins. As a matter of fact I happen to know he even enjoys the zeppelins . . . Well, sir, why not? Searchlights in the sky and a lot of lovely bangs, what more can any child want? . . . I'm not being callous, sir, Denis told me himself . . . Yes, he told me that Nannie makes him put in his prayers "God keep the zeppelins away" and he cheats every night and says under his breath "God don't you do anything of the kind" . . . (*Alarmed.*) No, sir, you mustn't . . . It's not blasphemy . . . No, sir, please don't. Please don't say a word to him. He wouldn't understand . . . Well, yes, if they do come, but you can take it from they won't . . . Goodnight.

He rings off, and is evidently a little put out by the conversation. A trifle abstractedly he opens the bedroom door, and calls.

It's all right now. I'm finished.

DAPHNE *comes back. He holds her chair for her as she sits.*

I'm so sorry for the interruption.

DAPHNE. No trouble at all, I assure you.

MARK. Excuse me, a moment. (*He goes to the window and, taking care of the black-out, peeps through the curtains.*)

DAPHNE *watches him steadily.*

I just wanted to see if there were any searchlights on.

DAPHNE. Got wind of something?

MARK. (*With his head through the curtains*). No, not wind exactly. Just something that was said on the telephone a moment ago, made me think of it. Not a sign of anything, as I thought. (*He comes back from the window.*)

While MARK *is arranging the next course,* DAPHNE *is staring hard at him.*

DAPHNE. Of course, now I don't just suspect, I think I know—(MARK *turns nervously with trifle poised.*)

MARK. Know what?

DAPHNE. You're thirty-two, you're not in uniform, sculptors aren't exempt I wouldn't suppose, and anyway, no one's ever made a living at just sculpture——

MARK. Oh, surely. Some people have, haven't they? Rodin for instance——

DAPHNE. Champagne and caviare?

MARK *places the dish before her.*

MARK. Oh, I should think so.

DAPHNE. (*Scornfully*). Don't tell me! I know the way artistical people live, and it's not like this. No, there's something else you don't want me to know about, but you needn't fuss, because I do.

MARK. Oh?

DAPHNE. You're Secret Service, aren't you?

MARK. Well——

DAPHNE. (*Interrupting*). That's all right, dear. I know you're not allowed to tell.

MARK. (*After a pause*). You think that Secret Service agents live on champagne and caviare?

DAPHNE. Oh yes, of course. Ever so well paid, I should think—what with the danger and all——

MARK. (*Lightly*). Oh, I don't know there's all that much danger, you know. Just a job, like any other.

DAPHNE. Don't tell me! I know what goes on. Well, it's really quite a thrill, isn't it? (*She gazes at him in awe and wonder.*)

MARK. You think spies are nice?

DAPHNE. Oh, *you're* not a spy. Germans are spies. British are agents. (*She continues to gaze at him, not touching her food.*)

MARK. Look, you're not eating your trifle,——

DAPHNE. Oh, I couldn't. I couldn't touch another thing. Excitement always gets me like that, you know—it goes straight to my stomach.

MARK. Oh, I'm so sorry. (*He gets up and hovers over her, a shade conscience-stricken.*) Look, supposing I were to tell you——

DAPHNE. (*Stopping her ears*). Oh, no—you mustn't tell me a thing. Not a thing. I know it's wrong. They shoot you for it.

He looks down at her in doubt. She smiles up at him. He gently takes her hands off her ears.

MARK. You don't have to stop your ears to what I'm going to tell you now, Daphne. I think you're the most enchanting and attractive and adorable creature in the world and if you would allow me to, I could be very, very fond of you.

DAPHNE. (*Gently*). Saucy, aren't you?

She closes her eyes and puts her head back in undisguised invitation. MARK *avails himself of it gently, at first, and then with warmth.*

MARK. (*Murmuring*). Daphne—my darling Daphne—

There is a sudden sharp noise at the window, as of a stone being thrown.

What was that?

DAPHNE. Sounded like a stone at the window.

There is the sound of a voice calling "Hi!" from the street outside.

Someone shouting too. (DAPHNE *rises.*)

VOICE. Hi!

MARK *crosses room quickly and goes to the window.*

MARK. Hullo, what is it?

VOICE. Is anyone there?

MARK. What?

VOICE. I'm looking for Daphne Prentice.

MARK. I can't hear.

MARK *draws the curtains and opens the window. The light has now gone from the sky.*

(*Out of the window*). What do you want?

VOICE. (*Off. In shrill, cockney tones*). I been ringing the bell and nothing happened.

MARK. Well, who are you? Go away!

VOICE. (*Off*). Is Daphne in there? Daph? Are you in there?

DAPHNE. (*In alarm*). Goodness gracious! It's Sidney.

MARK. Who's Sidney?

DAPHNE. My young brother. Oh, dear! I wonder what it is. Could you let him in, Mr Wright?

MARK. I suppose so.

He leans out of window.

Here, catch.

He throws a bunch of keys.

The big one's the downstairs door. It's Flat No 2 on the first floor.

SYDNEY. (*Off*). Right Ho!

DAPHNE. Well, I never. What could he be wanting?

MARK. I suppose he's not expecting to come to supper too, is he?

DAPHNE. Well, I don't know, I'm sure. Perhaps every-one's out at home and he felt lonely——

MARK. Oh, dear——

DAPHNE. Oh, he's such a clever little boy, doing ever so well for his age, Mr Wright. He's in munitions now.

MARK. Is he? (*The front door is heard to slam.*) Oh, there he is.

DAPHNE. You'll like him ever so much, I know.

MARK. I'm sure I shall.

MARK *opens doors. Sidney comes in, gives* MARK *his keys, then confronts* DAPHNE.

DAPHNE. Sidney! What are you doing here?

SIDNEY. Dad says you're to come home. Mum's back unexpected and she's creating——

DAPHNE. (*Angrily*). Oh, really! Isn't Mum awful! What— is she in one of her moods, or something?

SIDNEY. Terrible. She told Dad if he wasn't careful 'is daughter'd grow up an old tart like Auntie Mabel.

DAPHNE. Oh Sidney, be quiet! (*Suddenly conscious of her social duties.*) Oh Mr Wright, I'm so sorry, but I'm sure you understand about these little family squabbles. (*Her tone changes as she turns back to her brother.*) Now listen, Sidney. You just go straight back to Mum and tell her she and Dad are making a fuss about nothing. Tell her I haven't even finished my dinner yet, and I'll come back when I'm ready and not before.

SIDNEY. Mum said I was to wait and see you home.

DAPHNE. That's ridiculous. Mr Wright will see me home —won't you, Mr Wright?

MARK. Of course.

SIDNEY. Mum said to remember what happened the last time, when Mr Pennyfeather saw you home.

DAPHNE. Oh, Sidney, really! (*She turns back to* MARK.) Well, I don't know what to say, I'm sure, Mr Wright. It rather looks as if I shall have to go, I'm afraid.

MARK. Oh, dear. I tell you what—I've got an idea. Why couldn't Sidney go back and say he hadn't been able to find the address?

SIDNEY. 'Cos it wouldn't be true.

MARK. You're a little lacking in creative imagination, aren't you?

DAPHNE. I really think I'd better go. Oh, it's ever so vexing. I *am* sorry. I'll get my hat. (*She goes into the bedroom.*)

MARK. Very well, my dear. If you must, you must, I suppose. Run and get a taxi, Sidney.

SIDNEY. What for?

MARK. To take your sister home in, of course.

SIDNEY. Who's going to pay for it?

MARK. *I* am going to pay for it.

SIDNEY. Why?

MARK. (*Taking* SIDNEY *out*). Never mind these abstruse questions of etiquette, Sidney. Just go and get that taxi. Turn right and right again and stand on the corner until one passes. (DAPHNE *re-appears from bedroom,* MARK *comes in.*)

MARK. I've just sent Sidney for a taxi.

DAPHNE. (*Anxiously*). Oh, I do hope you didn't take seriously what Sidney let out about Mr Pennyfeather.

MARK. My dear, I can assure you, Mr Pennyfeather is the least of my worries at the moment. I'm only so upset that our evening should have ended so unsatisfactorily.

DAPHNE. Oh, well—there *are* other evenings, aren't there?

MARK. I hope so. Oh, indeed I hope so.

He kisses her.

Damn Sidney.

DAPHNE. It's Mum you should damn. Not little Sidney.

MARK. Having met little Sidney I prefer to damn little Sidney. (H*e turns to the door.*) I'll just slip along to the kitchen and leave a note for the servant. (*At the door.*) I suppose we couldn't take two taxis, one for Sidney and one for ourselves?

DAPHNE. Well—it might look a little odd, mightn't it?

MARK. No odder than the other alternative, which is to take one taxi and put Sidney on the roof.

He goes out, leaving doors open.

DAPHNE, *left alone, heaves a sigh, then sits on sofa and puts her hat on dejectedly. A door slams off and a very vivid lady* (ETHEL) *appears, in evening dress of extremely daring style, and a face like an exotic mask. She has evidently opened the front door with a latch key, because she is slipping it into her bag on entering. She nods pleasantly at* DAPHNE, *who has risen, alarmed at the apparition.*

ETHEL. Hot, isn't it?

DAPHNE. Yes, it is, isn't it. Quite sultry, really——

Her voice trails into astonished silence as she gazes at ETHEL *who has wandered over to a cupboard which she now opens as if from long practice and from which she brings a bottle of whisky and a tumbler. She pours out quite deliberately about a third of a tumblerful of the whisky, and then, with little finger genteelly curled, lifts her veil. Suddenly in one vast swallow she flings the drink down her gullet. No expression whatever crosses her countenance as she waits for a moment, savouring the drink. Then she politely holds out the bottle towards* DAPHNE.

ETHEL. (*With eyebrows courteously raised*). Do you indulge?

DAPHNE. Oh, no—thank you ever so.

ETHEL *nods pleasantly and pours herself out another vast drink. Holding it undrunk, at the moment, she wanders to mantle-piece. Then she takes a cigarette from a box and prepares to light it.*

DAPHNE. Excuse me asking, won't you—but would you mind telling me who you are?

ETHEL. (*As if that explained everything*). Ethel.

DAPHNE. Oh. Well, I'm sorry, but I'm afraid you'll have to tell me more than that. Haven't you got a sur-name?

ETHEL. (*After due thought*). Yes.

DAPHNE. What is it—if I might make so bold?

ETHEL. Skeffington-Rivers, I think. Yes. I'm almost sure it's that. (*She flings back her drink, puts the glass and bottle back in the cupboard, and wanders to the bedroom door. Conversationally.*) They say he went to Borneo.

She smiles vaguely and politely at DAPHNE *and drifts into the bedroom.*

DAPHNE. (*Aghast*). Well!

MARK *comes in from the hall.*

MARK. There we are, that's done.

DAPHNE. Well, really, Mr Wright, you have some very funny friends—I have to say.

MARK. Oh?

DAPHNE. Who was that woman who's just gone into your bedroom?

MARK. Has a woman just gone into my bedroom?

DAPHNE. Certainly. What's more she carried on as if she owned the whole flat—she had a latch key, too——

MARK. Oh, did she tell you her name?

DAPHNE. Well—she didn't seem quite sure of her surname, but her Christian name was Ethel.

MARK. Ethel? Ethel? (*Suddenly realising.*) Oh Lord! Ethel! (*After a moment of doubt, he laughs.*) That's easily explained. Ethel isn't my friend at all. In fact I've never met her—

DAPHNE. Then what's she doing wandering about your flat—making free with your whisky and——

MARK. She's a friend of Oscar Philipson. He's a friend of mine who usually stays here when he's on leave. I suppose he must have given her a latch key.

DAPHNE. It's very careless of him, I must say. He's not on leave now, though, is he?

MARK. No, he's not. But I expect——

He breaks off as there comes a noise from the hall.

OSCAR. (*Off*). All right, cabby. No, don't bring them in. Stick them down there. My man will look after them. Goodnight. Thank you.

There is the sound of the front door slamming.

MARK. This only goes to show, my dear, how wrong one can sometimes be. It appears that Oscar Philipson *is* on leave.

OSCAR PHILIPSON *comes in. Three years older than* MARK, *he is dressed in the uniform* (*Captain's*) *of the Coldstream Guards.*

OSCAR. (*With surprise*). Hullo, Mark. This is extremely good of you, I must say. How did you know?

MARK. I didn't know, that's just the trouble.

They shake hands.

C

(*Bitterly*). Why on earth didn't you warn Williams?

OSCAR. Oh. Didn't I?

MARK. No, you didn't, you idiot. It's an absolutely lunatic way to behave, suddenly to arrive on leave in the middle of the night like this without warning anybody at all.

OSCAR. But it's not the middle of the night. It's 8.35 exactly. And anyway I wired Ethel. Has she turned up?

MARK. Yes. She's in there.

OSCAR. Good.

MARK. But why did you only wire Ethel? Why didn't you wire me?

OSCAR. Well, I hope you'll forgive me saying so, old chap, but after six months in the trenches I thought that Ethel might provide the more convivial evening.

MARK. I see. Well, now, let me introduce Miss Prentice— Captain Philipson.

OSCAR. (*Eyeing her appreciatively*). How do you do?

DAPHNE. Pleased to meet you.

MARK. (*Meaningly*). Miss Prentice and I have been having a little dinner here—in my flat——

OSCAR. In your——

MARK. (*Firmly cutting him short*). Miss Prentice, incidentally, has been very kind about my flat, haven't you, Daphne?

DAPHNE. Oh, yes. I think it's ever such a nice flat——

OSCAR. Splendid.

MARK. Well, anyway, as I was saying, Miss Prentice and I have been having a little dinner here—in my——

OSCAR. Yes. I've got as far as that. Go on.

MARK. And only a moment or two ago we were talking about you. I was telling her how you always stay here when you're on leave.

OSCAR. Yes, I do, don't I?

MARK. And she thought it was rather careless of you to

let people like Ethel have a latch key to my flat, but I
said—or was going to say—that I didn't mind, because
you and I have always been such very close friends ever
since Eton—and in fact it was really you who made me
take up sculpture as a profession—

OSCAR. (*Listening very carefully*). Ah, yes. How well I
remember that.

MARK. You always had faith in me as a sculptor, didn't
you, Oscar?

OSCAR. Profound.

MARK. I remember him saying to me once—I know that
the name of Mark Wright is going to be famous one
day. People will nudge each other in the street and say
—there goes Mark Wright—the sculptor.

OSCAR. (*Slowly and understandingly*). And on the front of
12, Wilbraham Terrace, there'll be a little plaque saying
"Mark Wright, the sculptor, once *owned* a flat here"—

MARK. That's it. That's what you said——

OSCAR. I thought so. Well, now—may I help myself to a
drink?

MARK. What? Oh yes, of course. Make this flat your own,
my dear Oscar. You always do, anyhow.

OSCAR. Thank you very much.

ETHEL *emerges from the bedroom.*

Ethel, my dear. How very pleasant to see you
again.

ETHEL *manages a faint and stately smile, and then extends
him her cheek to kiss in the most sisterly manner.*

You've met the assembled company, haven't you?

ETHEL. The lady, yes. The gentleman is quite new to me.

OSCAR. Oh. This is Mark Wright—the famous sculptor.
This is Ethel . . .? Ethel! Now I've got a wonderful
idea. It's such a hot night—why don't you two ladies go
and cool yourselves in the garden, for a moment—
while I have a word with Mark——

MARK. Well—the fact is Miss Prentice and I were just on the point of leaving. Her brother has gone for a taxi——

OSCAR. (*Puzzled*). Her brother?

MARK. Yes. Her little brother, Sidney.

OSCAR. Well, well. We'll straighten that out later. Still, I'm afraid, Miss Prentice, whatever Mark says, Ethel and I can't allow you both to dash off like this—on the very first night of my leave. You must at least stay and help me crack a bottle of champagne.

Now, Ethel—take Miss Prentice and show her the garden by moonlight—(*To* MARK.) You don't mind Ethel showing Miss Prentice your garden by moonlight, do you, old chap?

MARK. Not a bit. I think it's a splendid idea——

DAPHNE. But do you think I should, really? Sidney'll be back any minute.

MARK. We can keep the taxi waiting. The fact is (*he lowers his voice.*) Oscar and I have something to discuss —of a very confidential nature.

DAPHNE. (*Light dawning*). Oh. Oh, I see. (*Indicating* OSCAR.) He's in the same line, is he?

MARK. Much the same line.

OSCAR. What line?

DAPHNE. That's all right, Captain Philipson, Mark hasn't given anything away—I assure you.

OSCAR. Oh. I'm glad to hear it.

DAPHNE. Come on, then, Mrs—er—come on. Let's see the garden.

The two girls go to the bedroom door.

ETHEL. After you.

DAPHNE *hesitates politely.*

No, I positively insist.

DAPHNE *goes out, followed by* ETHEL. OSCAR *after a glance at* MARK, *runs out after them.*

OSCAR. (*Off*). Ethel. Just a word in your ear——

After a moment he reappears.

I thought I'd better inform Ethel of the change in tenancy. Now before we go any further just exactly *what* line are you and I supposed to be in together?

MARK. The Secret Service.

OSCAR. I thought you were a sculptor.

MARK. I'm both.

OSCAR. Well, well. You've been cutting quite a dash, haven't you? You're not a famous matinée idol by any chance, or the open golf champion or the English Nijinsky?

MARK. No. You know it all. What do you think of her?

OSCAR. Very charming. Of course she's Sylvia again. (*He indicates the bronze head.*)

MARK. Yes. Extraordinary how like, isn't it?

OSCAR. It's mad how you go stampeding through life always looking for that same face. You're not in love with her are you?

MARK. My dear Oscar, I think she's enchanting, but only as a romantic pastime, not a serious undertaking.

OSCAR. I'm always terrified of the disaster than looms ahead for a character like you who refuses to come out of the emotional nursery. Still in love with the girl he met at seventeen. You know what you are, Mark, don't you? You're an emotional Peter Pan.

MARK. Well, what's wrong with that? I prefer to keep my emotions adolescent. They're far more enjoyable than adult ones.

OSCAR. So now after all this time as a faithful husband you've suddenly decided to become an amorist have you? An amorist, you!

MARK. Well, why not?

OSCAR. You haven't the talent my dear fellow. Go back to being a faithful husband I implore you and leave this difficult and dangerous pastime to us trained bachelors.

MARK. Dog in the manger.

OSCAR. I scorn that. We bachelors welcome competition from married men. We so much enjoy watching them come the inevitable cropper.

MARK. There won't be any cropper, Oscar. You talk as if I were a libertine and a sensualist like yourself. I'm not. I'm a romantic, and I intend in future to give full vent to my romanticism.

OSCAR. How far has this Prentice thing gone?

MARK. No distance at all. Thanks to Mum being in one of her moods——

OSCAR. Mum trouble, eh? That's bad. I'd rather Dad trouble, any day. But Mum trouble that's very bad.

MARK. Mum is no obstacle, I shall square Mum.

OSCAR. You will square Mum? Pardon me while I snigger. Don't you realise, you poor tyro, that the process of squaring Mum is one of the most difficult, intricate and dangerous operations in the whole field of amorism? And how, may I ask, do you propose to set about squaring Mum?

MARK. I haven't thought yet.

OSCAR. Oh, well. I suppose if you are really set on this perilous course, I shall have to give you a little tuition. What's the girl's telephone number?

MARK. I've no idea.

OSCAR. You've no idea. How typical! (*There is the noise of a stone at the window.*) My God! What's that?

MARK. Sidney. That's his usual way of announcing himself.

OSCAR. How old is Sidney?

MARK. About fifteen from the look of him. (*At window.*) That you Sidney?

SIDNEY. (*Off*). Hi!

MARK. Yes, I thought so. Here catch. (MARK *throws down the keys to* SIDNEY.)

OSCAR. All right, you go and collect the girls and leave
   Sidney to me.

MARK. I beg your pardon.

OSCAR. I'll square Sidney.

MARK. You'll square Sidney?

OSCAR. What's the matter, what sort of a little boy is
   he?

MARK. Oh, you'll like him very much. He's a very clever
   little boy, making lots of money in munitions and—(*A
   door is heard slamming off.*) My God, there he is! (MARK
   goes into the bedroom as SIDNEY *enters.*)

OSCAR. Hullo, my little man. Got the taxi?

SIDNEY. I've been ringing half a bleedin' 'our. Don't no
   one ever answer a bell in this 'ouse—all gone deaf or
   somethin'?

OSCAR. Quite a little wag, I see. Now, Sidney, how would
   you like to make half a crown, eh?

SIDNEY. What for?

OSCAR. To keep your nasty little trap shut.

SIDNEY. —'Oo are you?

OSCAR. Never mind who I am. What about it,
   Sidney?

SIDNEY. (*After a pause*). Cost you five bob.

OSCAR. Three and six, not a penny more.

SIDNEY. Five bob.

OSCAR. All right. All right—five bob it is. War profi-
   teer! Now go straight home and tell your Dad that you
   found the flat all right, but rang the bell and rang and
   rang and nobody came to the door. Don't tell him any
   more than that and you'll be telling the truth, won't
   you, Sidney—which will make quite a nice change for
   you. Now have you understood that?

SIDNEY. Where's my five bob.

OSCAR. There you are.

SIDNEY. Thanks. Tootaloo! (*He goes out.*)

OSCAR. (*Shouting after him*). And may the cigarettes you buy with it give you nicotine poisoning.

OSCAR *crosses to window.*

Hullo—cabby!

MARK *and the two girls have come in.*

ETHEL. And from that moment she was never the same again.

OSCAR. (*To cab driver*). Would you wait a moment. We're just coming out.

MARK. Oh, wasn't she?

ETHEL. Never the same again.

OSCAR. Oh, Miss Prentice, did Mark tell you? He had an idea that we might all four go out together to the Savoy —and do a little dancing——

DAPHNE. Oh, dear, I can't I'm afraid. You see, my family's expecting me back any minute.

OSCAR. Now let's cope with the family trouble. What's your telephone number, Miss Prentice?

DAPHNE. You can get us on Bayswater 4302, that's the newsagents downstairs.

OSCAR. Thank you. (*Into telephone.*) Hullo . . . Bayswater 4302, please.

DAPHNE. (*To* MARK, *alarmed*). Oh, dear—do you think he should? I don't want to get into hot water.

MARK. I shouldn't worry too much. He's very experienced in these things, you know.

OSCAR. I may have to tell your Mother a few half truths, Miss Prentice. I hope you won't mind——

DAPHNE. Oh, dear——

OSCAR. (*Into telephone*). Hullo . . . Oh, could I speak to Mrs Prentice, please? Yes, I'll wait.

DAPHNE. And anyway I couldn't go to the Savoy in a day dress, could I?

OSCAR. The dress problem I think we can cope with. Ethel has a large wardrobe, haven't you, Ethel?

ETHEL. It could be larger.

OSCAR. Yes. And I have no doubt it will be before my leave's much older. (*Into telephone.*) Is that Mrs Prentice? This is Brigadier-General Mason speaking. We've never met, I'm afraid, but a friend of mine called Mark Wright—you know—the sculptor—has brought your daughter round to my flat to a little informal party I'm giving here . . . Oh no, really? . . . Oh dear . . . Well, then I'm afraid he's probably been ringing Wright's doorbell and hasn't been able to get a reply. It's just as well I called then, isn't it? (*He laughs easily.*) Poor little Sidney! I'm so sorry . . . Oh no. Surely not, Mrs Prentice? Not this minute? She's so enjoying herself. Oscar Philipson is just going to sing . . . Oscar Philipson, the baritone . . . Yes. And I'm particularly anxious for her to meet a fellow who's coming in later— you may have heard of him—Lord St. Neots. He's in the Foreign Office.

MARK *starts violently.* DAPHNE *giggles.*

    I think it might be useful to your daughter to meet him . . . Oh, that *is* kind of you, Mrs Prentice. Just an hour or so . . . Yes . . . Would you like to speak to your daughter? . . . Here she is.

DAPHNE *fluttering takes the receiver from him.*

DAPHNE. (*Into receiver*). Hullo, Mum . . . Yes. It's lovely here . . . Oh, he's ever so nice . . . The Brigadier-General? Oh, yes, he's ever so nice, too . . . Yes, Mum, and there's ever such a nice lady I've been talking to called—er— Mrs Winnington-Piggot, I think. We've become great chums . . . Yes, Mum. All right . . . cheerioh, chin, chin. Nighty-night. (*She rings off and heaves a sigh of relief. To Oscar.*) Well, really, Captain—you were wonderful. You really were—I've never known Mum sound so good tempered——

OSCAR. (*Carelessly*). Oh, it was nothing really. Nothing at all. (*He meets* MARK's *eyes, which are fixed rather crossly on him and bows slightly.*)

DAPHNE. However did you think of that silly name—Lord—what was it?

OSCAR. St Neots. I don't know. It just sprang to my lips somehow. Well, go on, girls. Jump in the taxi, get dressed up at Ethel's place, and meet us at the Savoy in half an hour.

DAPHNE. Oo lovely, lovely, lovely! What a thrill! Come on, Ethel. (*She collects her things and dashes to the door.* ETHEL *follows more impassively.*)

ETHEL. What's your style, dear?

DAPHNE. Well, I don't really know, dear. It's more a question of size than of style. But I should think something simple—what have you got?

ETHEL. I'm afraid I may find it rather difficult to lay my hands on anything very *simple*—but let me see, now, I have got a flame-coloured spangled satin, with a rather virginal line to the neck——

Their voices fade as the front door bangs.

MARK. (*Explosively*). It was all nonsense what you said about my being emotionally adolescent. After seven years of married life all sorts of mysterious forces and pressures go rumbling around inside one. At any moment there might have been a catastrophic explosion. But now I've found the safety valve. A double life. It's a wonderful idea, Oscar, you know, wonderful. I wonder why more people haven't thought of it.

OSCAR. Quite a few people have. You obviously don't read the right Sunday papers.

MARK. Tell me, Oscar, how much are you paying for this flat?

OSCAR. Two-fifty a year.

MARK. Would you take five hundred furnished?

OSCAR. Certainly not.

MARK. Seven-fifty then.

OSCAR. No, don't go any higher. I'd have to accept.

MARK. Eight hundred.

OSCAR. It's fatal, you know, Mark. It'll end in the most terrible sordid tragedy. I can see the headlines now— "Viscount's love-nest raided. Incredible disclosures". Think of your poor wife, and young Denis, Mark. Do you want Williams?

MARK. Yes.

OSCAR. That'll be another two hundred.

MARK. Done.

OSCAR. Oh dear, oh dear! My poverty but not my will consents. Merchant of Venice.

MARK. Romeo and Juliet. Of course you can stay here whenever you want.

OSCAR. Seriously, Mark, and at the risk of being a bore— it'll never work. You really can't hope to have the best of your two worlds. They'll collide and blow each other up. Mark Wright blown up would be a good thing, but I'm not keen on seeing Mark St Neots in little pieces.

MARK. There's no reason why they should ever conflict. I intend to keep my two worlds rigidly separate.

OSCAR. You can't, you can't. Nature will take her revenge —you mark my words.

MARK. Stop talking like a character out of Thomas Hardy. What was that? (*He gets up and suddenly stops on his way to the door.*)

We now hear it too. Whistles are being distantly blown, and there is the distant sound of shouting. Suddenly a voice shouts clearly in the street outside: "Take cover! Take cover!"

OSCAR. Zeppelins!

MARK. Oh, my God! Of all things to happen now. Denis' prayers have been answered.

OSCAR. What are you burbling about?

MARK. Look, Oscar, I'll join you at the Savoy later. I've got to go home first.

OSCAR. Why, for heaven's sake?

MARK. I can't explain now, but Denis needs protection.

OSCAR. From the bombs do you mean?

MARK. No. From his old imbecile of a grandfather. He'll give the poor boy hell—I must run. Just in case I get caught at home, and can't get away, explain to Daphne, will you? Tell her I'll telephone her tomorrow—(*He is half out of the door when he notices* OSCAR *is laughing.*) What are you laughing at?

OSCAR. Your two worlds. Rigidly separate!

MARK. (*Furiously*). This, let me tell you, is only an isolated incident—a purely fortuitous circumstance. It proves nothing—absolutely nothing. (OSCAR *continues to laugh.*) Damn you, Oscar.

MARK *dashes out.*

CURTAIN

ACT II

SCENE: *The same. Before the curtain rises, a small jazz band can be heard playing a tune of the period ("Makin' Whoopee"). The curtain rises and the band can now be determined as coming from the party in progress downstairs. The sound of voices joins the music from the band.*

The year is now 1929 and the time is about 6.30 of an afternoon in late Spring.

The room has undergone some changes since 1917. New curtains and covers show a feminine influence (of the "jazz school") and a rearrangement of the furniture has entirely removed the rather austerely celibate air that the room once had.

At the rise of the curtain, WILLIAMS—*older by thirteen years, but dressed, as ever, in a neat blue serge suit—with a white jacket—is at the telephone. He is humming "Makin' Whoopee")*

WILLIAMS. Sloane 7838? . . . This is the Foreign Office. Could I speak to Lady Binfield, please . . . Oh, that is Lady Binfield speaking? Foreign Office here . . . I'm just ringing . . .

*The door opens and a girl (*BUBBLES*) in a very short skirt and a very boyish bob appears.*

BUBBLES. (*Vaguely to* WILLIAMS). Hullo?

WILLIAMS. (*Sharply*). Don't come in here, Miss. The party's downstairs in the studio and shut the door, please! (*He holds his hand over the mouthpiece.*)

BUBBLES. Caveman! (*She disappears, closing the door behind her, dispelling some of the noise.*)

WILLIAMS. (*Into telephone*). Lady Binfield? . . . I'm so very sorry. It was a dispatch coming in . . . I'm speaking for

Lord Binfield. He hadn't time to call you himself. He's had to go very suddenly to Cheltenham on urgent business . . . Cheltenham . . . Two or three days, I believe . . . Well, of course, I wouldn't know that, being only a clerk, but I expect it'll be something to do with the Disarmament Conference . . . Yes, Lady Binfield . . . No, I'm afraid I can't give you his number. It's confidential . . . Well of course, I might be able to get a message to him if it's urgent . . . It is . . . Very well, I'll see what I can do . . . to ring you immediately. I see. Thank you, Lady Binfield. Goodbye.

BUBBLES *reappears at the double doors.*

BUBBLES. Hullo! My dear, haven't we met some place before?

WILLIAMS. I told you miss, the party's downstairs in the studio.

BUBBLES. I know, I just came from there. Blissful, my dear, utterly blissful, but my dear, no Vodka.

WILLIAMS. All right, miss, if you'll go back I'll slip out and buy you a bottle—but guests aren't really supposed to come up here.

BUBBLES. (*Hugging him*). You're a gorgeous beast, (*Kisses him.*) and I love you in that off-white affair. What's in there? (*Pointing at bedroom door.*) Instinct tells me a bed.

WILLIAMS. Miss Patterson's in there dressing, miss. If I might suggest——

BUBBLES. Goody. Goody. (*She flings open the bedroom door.*) Nora, angel dear, you're giving a simply thrillsome party. Why aren't you at it?

NORA. (*Off*). Go away, Bubbles, I'm in a draught.

BUBBLES. Darling, may I use your delicious bed for just a sec. Baby has a tiny migraine and she feels she'd be better on her back.

NORA. Isn't that the way Baby usually feels? All right, come in.

BUBBLES. Angel! (*To* WILLIAMS.) Well, goodbye, darling.
It's been simply divine meeting you.

She goes into the bedroom. WILLIAMS, *with a disapproving*
sigh, goes to the sideboard to pick up a tray. OSCAR *comes in.*
In civilian clothes he looks extremely elegant, but has put on
a little weight round the girth.

OSCAR. (*Extending his hand*). Hullo, Williams.

WILLIAMS. Hullo, Colonel.

OSCAR. Delighted to see you again.

WILLIAMS. How are you?

OSCAR. Oh, very fit, thank you. Very fit.

WILLIAMS. You're looking very fit. You've put on a bit of
weight, haven't you?

OSCAR. No. (*He pulls his stomach in instinctively.*)

WILLIAMS. I thought, perhaps, just a little round here—
(*he indicates his stomach.*)

OSCAR. Nonsense. An optical illusion. Back to the light.
Most deceptive. (*He puts his hat and stick on the table*
in the window.)
Well, where's the party?

WILLIAMS. You passed it, sir, on the way up. Didn't you
hear it?

OSCAR. That bedlam downstairs?

WILLIAMS. That's right, sir, in the studio.

OSCAR. Studio?

WILLIAMS. His Lordship's taken the flat downstairs and
made it into a studio, sir.

OSCAR. Good Lord. What does he want a studio for?

WILLIAMS. To sculpt in, I think. Miss Patterson's idea, of
course. Very artistically minded, Miss Patterson. She's
got a job all right now, sir—walking on in that new
play at the Strand——

OSCAR. Tell me, Williams, what's she like?

WILLIAMS. Well, sir, I never was much of a one for the
bright young people.

OSCAR. It rather depends how bright the young people are·

WILLIAMS. (*The sound of piano playing mixes with the voices coming from the party*). I shouldn't think they come much brighter than Miss Patterson. Take this party of hers. Well, sir, you'd hardly credit the way they carry on downstairs. Talk about the last days of Pompeii. That reminds me. I must get back or I'll get stick——

OSCAR. That's it Williams. Over the top.

WILLIAMS. It *is* over the top and no perishing mistake. You coming, sir?

OSCAR. I suppose so. (*Stopping.*) Oh, before I enter the fray—it *is* still Mr Wright, is it, Williams?

WILLIAMS. That's right, sir. Mark Wright, 12, Wilbraham Terrace, and the Savage Club. That's what's on the cards.

OSCAR. Good Lord. Mr Wright has cards now, has he?

WILLIAMS. Oh yes, sir. Everything quite *comme il fait*——

The bedroom door is kicked open and NORA *emerges, without shoes and fiddling with the buttons of her dress. She turns her back to* OSCAR *who is standing nearer the bedroom door than* WILLIAMS, *when she speaks.*)

NORA. Do me up, darling, would you? I can't reach——

OSCAR. Oh, yes. Delighted. (*He fiddles with the buttons.*)

NORA. (*To* WILLIAMS). Better make some black coffee for Miss Fairweather, Williams.

WILLIAMS. Miss Fairweather, miss?

NORA. The pass-out case on my bed. (*To* OSCAR.) It's too shaming you know, poor Bubbles—I forgot she could only drink Vodka. Gin always flies straight to her head.

OSCAR. (*Still fiddling with the buttons*). Indeed? And where does the Vodka usually fly to?

NORA. You'd be surprised. Or would you?

He fixes her dress.

Thank you, darling, you're an angel.

She goes back into the bedroom.

OSCAR. Tiens, tiens.

WILLIAMS. Exactly, sir.

OSCAR. Tell me, Williams, what happened to that nice Miss—what was her name?

WILLIAMS. Miss Sprigg? Same as usual, sir—got too interested—wanted to see him too often. You know the form.

OSCAR. I know the form.

WILLIAMS. She's got a hat shop now—calls herself Dahlia. His Lordship bought it for her, of course. Doing well with it, too. Quite friends they are still—but—well— you know—friends are one thing, and the other thing's the other thing, isn't it?

OSCAR. I have based my life on that belief, Williams.

MARK *comes in. He has hardly changed, except for a very slight greying of the hair.*

MARK. Williams—what are you doing gossiping up here? You're needed downstairs. Hullo, Oscar.

OSCAR. Hullo, Mark.

WILLIAMS. Sorry, my Lord. I was just getting some black coffee for a Miss Fairweather.

MARK. A Miss who?

WILLIAMS. Guest that's been taken queer—in there——

MARK. Oh—and Williams, there's a man down there with grey hair and a red face and a moustache. Colonel some-body or other. He's been shouting, "Hullo Binfield", across the room at me. Get him out, somehow. Spill a shaker on him, or something——

WILLIAMS. I'll try, my Lord.

MARK. And Williams—did you call my home?

WILLIAMS. Yes, my Lord. Her Ladyship said you were to ring her most particular. Something very urgent, she said.

MARK. Where exactly am I supposed to be today?

WILLIAMS. Cheltenham, sir.

D

MARK. I see. What's the procedure, Williams, for making a trunk call?

WILLIAMS. Well, my Lord, I suggest you get Colonel Philipson to call the number, and say, "Cheltenham wants you", leave three seconds, make a click and then speak yourself.

OSCAR. How do we make the three pips?

WILLIAMS. I think it would be better to keep it under the three minutes. The three pips are a bit risky. I tried it once but her Ladyship said there's a silly woman on the line saying "peep". (WILLIAMS *goes.*)

MARK. Well, Oscar. How was Egypt?

OSCAR. Hot.

MARK. Are you back for good?

OSCAR. No. Only a month—damn it.

MARK. I don't know why you don't give it up. There's no future in soldiering. We diplomats are going to see to it there's not going to be another war.

OSCAR. My dear chap, you don't give up the Brigade of Guards. You talk as if I were in the Army or something.

MARK. My God, you have grown a paunch, haven't you?

OSCAR. It isn't a paunch. I can pull it in. Look. (*He does so.*)

MARK. Then it comes out there.

He points, with some truth, to OSCAR's *over-expanded chest. Then he walks over to* OSCAR *and extends his own rather impressively straight stomach.*

Feel that.

OSCAR. (*Doing so*). Oh well, of course, if you wear a corset——

MARK. A support—which has nothing whatever in common with a corset—is a healthy and sensible garment for a man who has reached the age of—thirty-five.

OSCAR. The age of what?

MARK. Thirty-five I said, and thirty-five I meant.

OSCAR. My poor dear old Mark, you can never hope to

get away with that. But damn it, if you're thirty-five, I'm thirty-eight. Well, I'm only three years older than you.

MARK. Four.

OSCAR. Three. It's March now. Now even I have never tried to get away with less than forty-two.

MARK. Yes. I think that's very wise of you. (*Into telephone*) Hullo, I want Sloane 7838 please. Now if that's plainly understood perhaps you'll be kind enough to give your famous imitation of Cheltenham on the telephone. (OSCAR *reluctantly goes to the telephone.*)

OSCAR. You thirty-five—with a hulking great son on the verge of being a diplomat.

MARK. He's not hulking and he's got a good four years to go yet before he's a diplomat. That's to say if he gets in.

OSCAR. (*Indicating telephone*). Engaged.

MARK. Damn it. Who on earth is she talking to?

OSCAR. Why shouldn't Denis get in? He's got brains, that boy. You mustn't underestimate my Godson.

MARK. He's a damn little slacker. He's been at this place in Tours for three months and he can't even write a line of a letter in reasonably correct French. Keeps complaining that the daughter of the house has fallen in love with him.

OSCAR. I don't understand what he has to complain about in that.

MARK. I'm sure you don't. But Denis, I am happy to tell you, has inherited his father's romantic nature.

OSCAR. Don't say he's acquired a Sylvia too, since I've been away.

MARK. A rather deplorable one, I'm afraid. Ursula Culpepper.

OSCAR. Ursula Culpepper? Oh, my God!

MARK. You know her? Off the stage, I mean——

oscar. It's hard not to know her, isn't it? His Uncle
Oscar will have to have a very severe word with him.
Oh dear, oh dear! What do these children see in her?

mark. Glamour, I suppose. She uses a lot of words very
loudly that they've only previously read chalked on walls.

oscar. An unsuitable Sylvia—I grant you.

mark. Exactly. I've put my foot down pretty hard, I may
say. I had to, of course. He won't see her again.

oscar. Good. Oh, by the way, Mark, congratulations on
your new appointment.

mark. Thanks. How did you hear?

oscar. It was in The Londoner's Diary. Didn't you read
it?

mark. No. What did it say?

oscar. Oh, something about Lord Binfield being our new
Minister in La Plaz.

mark. Oh. Nothing else?

oscar. No. I don't think there was anything else.

mark. (*Nastily*). Oh, wasn't there? Well, then, perhaps
this will refresh your memory. (*He takes a newspaper
cutting from his pocket. Reading.*) "The Earl of Binfield, a
well-known and popular figure in Brussels, where he has
been our Counsellor of Embassy since 1926 . . ."

oscar. You said you hadn't read it——

mark. Well, I have! "is today to be congratulated on a
new appointment fitting to his brilliant attainments."

oscar. (*Sulkily*). All right, all right, I remember.

mark. How does it go on?

oscar. Oh, something about your being thin——

mark. (*Reading*). "Slim. Slim, handsome and witty, Lord
Binfield, who inherited the title from his father in
1923——"

oscar. Yes, yes. I'll try that number again. (*He goes to the
telephone.*) Get me Sloane 7838 please. Friend of yours
this Londoner fellow, I presume?

MARK. Never met the man in my life. (*He puts the cutting away.*)

OSCAR. They said something like that about me once.

MARK. What did they say?

OSCAR. Oh—something about being one of the best-looking officers in the Brigade of Guards—you know—something rather embarrassing like that. (*Hastily.*) Oh is that—I mean are you—er—(*Prompted by* MARK.) Sloane 7838 . . . You are. Splendid. Br—er—Cheltenham—that's it—Cheltenham wants you . . . hold on.

MARK, *after glaring at* OSCAR, *takes the receiver.*

(*Whispering frantically*). Click! Click!

MARK. (*Whispering back*). Click off. (*Into receiver after a pause.*) Hullo? Hullo, darling . . . Can you hear me all right? . . . Yes, I can hear you. They tell me you were trying to get hold of me. Oh, my God . . . is he there? Well, where is he? . . . Well, why did you let him? . . . Game of squash, I don't think. More likely drinking in a Bloomsbury bar, with Ursula Culpepper and her crowd of degenerates.

OSCAR. Denis?

MARK. Yes. (*Into receiver.*) Is he deigning to come back to dinner? . . . You don't think so. That's charming . . . Sorry for him? Well, I can assure you you're going to be a good deal sorrier for him when I get through with him . . . Well, what do you expect me to do? Pat him on the back and say, well done, little man. Ruin your career. I'm proud of you? Well, it's going to be difficult for me, but I shall come up first thing tomorrow morning—even if it's only for a few hours—No. I can't tonight . . . No. Utterly impossible. You can tell him from me he's not going to enjoy the interview, and he'd better buy his ticket back to Tours first thing in the morning . . . Goodbye . . . Victorian? . . . really, what a ridiculous—Hullo, hullo.

He takes the receiver from his ear and replaces it slowly. The sound of the party is heard.

Victorian. Me?

OSCAR. At thirty-five.

MARK. Shut up. (*Morosely.*) The damn little fool!

OSCAR. Done a bunk?

MARK. Doesn't like it over there. Decided he's going to be an actor.

OSCAR. Oh. Can he act?

MARK. No, of course not.

OSCAR. How do you know?

MARK. I've seen him.

OSCAR. What as?

MARK. Shylock.

OSCAR. What was he like?

MARK. Unspeakable.

OSCAR. Well, perhaps he wasn't very well cast.

MARK. (*Aggressively*). Are *you* taking his side against me too?

OSCAR. (*Hastily*). No, no. It's just that—well, after all, there are always two sides to every question, aren't there?

MARK. Who the hell says so?

OSCAR. (*Pacifically*). No one says so, old chap. It's just that it's a sort of—generally accepted theory——

MARK. Well, it's a damn silly theory. My God, the way they allow these boys to act in these plays at school is a positive scandal. Filling their heads with all sorts of dangerous subversive ideas——

OSCAR. (*Reminiscently*). Come to think of it, I was rather good as Lady Macbeth.

MARK. (*Viciously*). You were ghastly as Lady Macbeth. You were absolutely excruciating as Lady Macbeth.

OSCAR. (*With dignity*). The Etonian said I took my part with spirit and courage——

MARK. The Etonian must have been out of its mind.

The door opens and NORA *emerges, dressed, very daringly, for the party. The strains of "Dance Little Lady" can be heard from downstairs.*

NORA. Oh hullo, darlings.

MARK. Oh, hullo, darling. I don't think you've met Oscar Philipson, have you? He's one of my very oldest and dearest friends——

NORA. No. How do you do?

OSCAR. As a matter of fact we met a moment ago.

NORA. Did we?

OSCAR. I was the one who did you up—do you remember?

NORA. Oh, my God, yes. A skilful and practised hand, I thought, too——

OSCAR. Oh, did you? That's very good of you.

NORA. Darling, it's too wonderful to meet you at last. I've heard so much about you from Mark.

OSCAR. Oh, you mustn't believe all that Mark says, you know.

NORA. My God, no. You're so right. I mean, from what he said, I thought you'd be quite old and staid and ordinary and, my God, look at you, a positive dream boat, my dear——

OSCAR. (*Delighted*). A dream boat? Oh, do you really think so——

NORA. An absolute Gondola, my dear. But what, I'm here to ask, are we all doing up here? I mean, isn't there a party on somewhere, or isn't there?

MARK. Oh, yes. It's still there, I think.

NORA. My God, without a host or hostess? It's too shaming for words. Why have you deserted your post, you wicked man?

MARK. Only under fire, my dear. There's a terrible man down there I've taken an acute dislike to——

NORA. Oh my dear, I'm sure there are a hundred terrible

men down there I'm going to take a positive, burning hatred to, but really that couldn't be less here or there, now, could it? Or could it? My darlings, let's fly to our deadly social duties this instant——

MARK. No, I'm not going down again until that Colonel's gone. Oscar, run down, would you, and see if he's still there?

OSCAR. Well, what does he look like?

MARK. Red-faced, grey hair, grey moustache, loud voice. You can't mistake him. He's the only one there even remotely the type.

OSCAR. (*At the door*). But—dash it all—I won't know anyone down there.

MARK. Yah! Windy!

OSCAR. (*Considering him*). Witty. Slim, handsome and witty. The Londoner! (*He makes a face and—departs.*)

NORA. What did he mean?

MARK. Some obscure joke. (*He kisses her.*) How are you? I haven't seen you for nearly three whole days.

NORA. Darling—devastated with mad expectancy for this wonderful week-end. (*Showing her dress.*) You haven't said yet?

MARK. Oh, is that the new get up?

She shows it off by walking up and down.

Oh yes. It's exquisite.

NORA. Quite an exquisite price too, darling. Does that matter?

He looks at her, smiling.

Or does it?

MARK. (*Embracing her*). It doesn't.

NORA. Mr Wright, I adore you. (*She holds his hands.*) Darling, you really must be madly rich——

MARK. Not *madly* rich.

NORA. But where do you get it all from, darling? Surely not out of sculpting?

MARK. Oh well. There's the other work, too, you know.

NORA. The Secret Service? But they pay you nothing in that—my dear—a positive pittance—I know. Look at Flossie Philips.

MARK. Flossie Philips?

NORA. Darling, you must know Flossie. She's terribly important in your little affair. X101 or some such madly gay number, and she has trouble even to get her bus-fares paid. So where, I'd like to know, darling, does all this gorgeous money, which I frankly dote on, come from?

MARK. Does it matter?

NORA. No. Not awfully. Madly mysterious you are, aren't you? But I'll find out, don't worry. Darling, what's all this lunacy about going to La Paz or somewhere?

MARK. Well, it's true, I'm afraid.

NORA. But why La Paz, for God's sake?

MARK. We're not allowed to choose where we're sent.

NORA. But, darling, La Paz! My God, it's the other end of the earth. Now Brussels wasn't so bad—you could get over for week-ends. But La Paz. You can't go to La Paz.

MARK. (*Tenderly*). Can't I?

NORA. No. Tell them you won't go. My God, there's far more Secret Service to be done in London than in La Paz. Tell them to keep you in London.

MARK. I've told them. They won't.

NORA. Then tell them to go to hell.

MARK. I've thought of that too.

NORA. Have you? On the level?

MARK. On the level.

NORA. Are you going to?

MARK. I don't know. It's a very big decision.

NORA. Can I help you to make it?

MARK. Yes.

NORA. How?

MARK. By looking at me as you are now.

NORA. Like Sylvia, you mean?

MARK. No. Not like Sylvia. Like Nora.

Pause.

NORA. You realise I must go down to my party, don't you?

MARK. Yes. But I also realise that later tonight you're
     going to look at me in the same way as you're doing
     now. (*After a pause he turns her to the door.*)

NORA. (*At the door*). Darling—I've got a wonderful idea.
     Why on earth didn't I think of it before——

MARK. What?

NORA. I'll get Flossie Philips to fix it.

MARK. (*Vehemently*). No, don't, for heaven's sake!

NORA. But, darling, one word from Flossie and you're in
     London for years——

MARK. Darling, one word from Flossie and I'm in Queer
     Street for life. No, Nora. Thank you very much, but
     we're really not supposed to talk about these things, and
     I can get into very serious trouble if you mention it.
     Be an angel. Not a word.

NORA. On one condition.

MARK. What?

NORA. You know.

Pause.

MARK. Then give me a truthful answer to a sincere question.

NORA. Right.

MARK. If I did that, would you stay with me for life?

Pause.

NORA. Yes.

MARK. Thank you. See you in a minute.

NORA *opens the door and lets in the sound of the party.*

NORA. (*Listening*). My God, it sounds as dead as a door-
     knob. I'd better get Babs to do her fan dance—if she's
     still vertical. Don't be long, darling.

She disappears. Almost simultaneously, BUBBLES, *tousled and shoeless, appears in the bedroom door, staring at* MARK *through half-closed eyes.*

BUBBLES. Has Ponsonby brought the Vodka yet?

MARK. (*Politely*). Who is Ponsonby? And what Vodka is he bringing?

BUBBLES. My good man—I am not here to bandy words with a complete stranger——

MARK. What are you here for?

BUBBLES. I've no idea. (*She disappears into the bedroom again and closes the door.*)

OSCAR *darts in through the hall door.*

OSCAR. (*In alarm*). My God, Mark—you know that Colonel of yours?

MARK. Yes?

OSCAR. I'm flying for my life.

MARK. Why?

OSCAR. Husband trouble.

MARK. Serves you right. You shouldn't have husband trouble at all. It's utterly against the rules.

OSCAR. The game I play—which is entirely of my own invention—has, happily—no rules of any kind. May I make myself a cocktail?

MARK. Why?

OSCAR. Well, I'm not going to get one downstairs, it seems.

MARK. Yes. All right. Everything's there. Make one for me too.

OSCAR. (*At the sideboard*). Luckily he's never seen me—this Colonel Wilberforce, but some idiot told him I was at the party, and now he's roaring across the room about having a word or two to say to this young rotter Philipson.

MARK. Young rotter? Oh well, of course, you were saying he'd never seen you.

OSCAR. And you tell me my humour is fourth form. There's no ice.

MARK. Of course there's no ice.

OSCAR. I used to keep it in a sort of vacuum thingammajig. What's happened to it?

MARK. You took it.

OSCAR. So I did. Well, as I was saying, this mutual menace of ours, this Colonel Wilberforce, has an entirely misguided notion that I once took certain liberties with Mrs Wilberforce in a taxi going from the Pyramids to the Cairo Opera House. (*He tries the cocktail.*) This tastes rather good. Do you know, I think it's better without ice.

MARK. How misguided was the Colonel's notion?

OSCAR. Oh, entirely. It wasn't in a taxi at all.

MARK. On a camel?

OSCAR. Fourth form. Fourth form. It was in a beautiful moonlit garden, and I didn't take liberties. I was accorded them.

MARK. God, what have you put in this thing? (*He indicates his cocktail which he has just sipped.*)

OSCAR. Ordinary gin and French. It's that little touch of lemon that makes the difference.

MARK. It's got a sort of sickly taste—like a decaying turnip.

OSCAR. Nonsense. It's delicious.

(*He drinks his down.* MARK *puts his aside.*)

MARK. Oscar—I've got something very serious to tell you. Can I have your whole attention, please? (OSCAR *nods. There is a pause.*) What do you think of her?

OSCAR. Her? Oh, charming, charming—Of course, she's Sylvia, version 1929—bang up to date.

MARK. Sylvia doesn't come into it this time.

OSCAR. Of course she does. This girl is the living image——

MARK. I know. It makes no difference. I'm not in love with an image. I'm in love with Nora Patterson.

OSCAR. I knew this would happen one day. You can't say I haven't warned you. Oh Lord—I suppose I shall have to give evidence.

MARK. Evidence? Where?

OSCAR. (*Crossing to sideboard for another drink*). At the divorce.

MARK. Divorce? Whose divorce?

OSCAR. Your divorce of course.

MARK. Don't be so infernally melodramatic. Who's talking about divorce?

OSCAR. You said you were in love with——

MARK. Well, so I am. All I'm trying to tell you is I'm sufficiently in love with her to give up the Diplomatic.

Pause.

OSCAR. Tiens, tiens.

MARK. What did you say?

OSCAR. I said, tiens, tiens. It's a French expression meaning hold, hold.

MARK. Have you any other comment?

OSCAR. Only that sitting on this very sofa—many years ago—I warned you of this very disaster—I remember it perfectly. Your two worlds, I said, will collide, and blow each other up. Mark Wright blown up, I said, will be a good thing. But Mark Binfield blown up, I said—will be a catast—catastrophe. Do you know—I think I did put something rather funny in this. (*He indicates his cocktail.*)

MARK. (*After sipping his own glass*). You know what you've done, don't you? You've put brandy in instead of vermouth.

OSCAR. Ridiculous. I couldn't have—(*He goes to the drink sideboard.*) There's the gin. And there's the—(*He sniffs the second decanter. Furiously.*) Well, of all the idiotic things to do—to go and put brandy in the vermouth decanter.

MARK. That's the brandy decanter. There's no such thing as a vermouth decanter.

OSCAR. Certainly there's such a thing as a vermouth decanter. This is the vermouth decanter. I always kept vermouth in this decanter—

MARK. Well, I keep brandy in it.

OSCAR. You realise what you've done, don't you? Quite apart from rendering me insensible hours before my normal time, you've very probably given me another of my livers. (*Bad temperedly.*) What were we talking about?

MARK. Me—giving up the Diplomatic.

OSCAR. Oh yes. Catastrophe. (*Surprised.*) I said it all right that time.

MARK. Nonsense.

OSCAR. (*Crossly*). I *did* say it all right——

MARK. I mean it's nonsense to sit there just burbling catastrophe.

OSCAR. (*Darkly*). You'll see, my boy. You'll see. Oh, and I have one further comment to make. A brief comment but one of extraordinary penetrative—penetrativeness——

MARK. Try penetration.

OSCAR. I've said penetrativeness now.

MARK. Make the comment.

OSCAR. Denis.

MARK. That's idiotic. Denis is eighteen. He can't possibly know his own mind, while I know exactly what I'm doing——

OSCAR. The difference, in fact, between suicide while of unsound mind and *felo de se*. Do you know that's rather good? I wish someone could have heard that.

MARK. I heard it, and thought it damn silly. Besides, Denis thinks he's going to be an actor——

OSCAR. What do you think you're going to be?

MARK. Myself. No more than that. I'll sculpt a bit more, perhaps—write a little—read all the books I ought to have read—

OSCAR. You can do all that in La Paz.

MARK. Yes, but why La Paz, for heaven's sake? Why should I, in the prime of life——

OSCAR. Slim, handsome and witty——

MARK. Shut up. Why should I incarcerate myself in a place like La Paz—probably for years and years— exiled, forgotten, humiliated, ignored—in some moth-eaten little South American dust-heap?

OSCAR. It's a delightful city, La Paz.

MARK. Have you been there?

OSCAR. I've had a postcard.

MARK. Minister in La Paz! I tell you, Oscar, if I give in now, I give in to old age, and dullness and respectability and drab security and all the things I've been trying to run away from in the last thirteen years—ever since I invented Mark Wright. Very well—the two worlds *have* collided—who cares? Better Binfield go under than Wright. Binfield is nothing—there are millions like him—respectable, domesticated, frustrated bores, half-dead without knowing it. But Wright is alive—he has a great capacity for living—and life should be lived in the full tide—not snoozed away in stagnant backwaters. I tell you, Oscar, I have reached my turning point—the moment that comes to a man once and only once in his lifetime—when he has to make a Napoleonic decision— a decision that is going to make or mar him for the rest of his time on earth. Well, I've made mine. I'm resigning from the Service tomorrow.

OSCAR *is staring at him fixedly.*

MARK. Well?

OSCAR. Extraordinary the way your eyebrows move about when you get excited.

MARK. Any further comment?

OSCAR. Yes.

MARK. What?

OSCAR. Disaster. Utter cata—disaster——

WILLIAMS *comes in with a tray on which is a coffee pot, a bottle and a cup.*

MARK. Has that damn Colonel gone yet?

WILLIAMS. No, my Lord. I spilled a tomato juice on him, like you said, but he hardly seemed to notice it. (*He goes into the bedroom.*)

MARK. What on earth can we do to get rid of him?

After a second's pause the same idea occurs to them simultaneously. They both turn and look at the shaker. They get up and go to the sideboard.

Can you remember the exact formula?

OSCAR. Of course. A perfectly ordinary dry Martini, my dear chap. (*He mixes a cocktail, using the same decanters as before.*) Two parts gin—one part vermouth—a touch more vermouth, I think, don't you—don't let's be stingy—and then—just a dash of lemon, which brings the whole thing to glorious life. There we are. (*He sips it.*) Yes. That is the veritable brew. The Philipson patent husband-remover or Binfield-shouter slayer.

WILLIAMS *emerges from the bedroom.* MARK *takes the shaker from* OSCAR *and hands it to* WILLIAMS.

MARK. Ah, Williams, this is for Colonel Wilberforce only. Only, understand.

WILLIAMS. Yes, my Lord.

MARK. But be careful. Don't spill it, or we'll have a hole in the floor.

OSCAR. What was it you just took into the bedroom, Williams?

WILLIAMS. Black coffee—and vodka—sir, for one of the guests.

OSCAR. Oh. What sex is the guest?

WILLIAMS. Female, sir

OSCAR. Below the age of thirty?

WILLIAMS. Yes, sir.

OSCAR. What is her name?

WILLIAMS. Oh! I heard Miss Patterson call her Bubbles.

OSCAR. Bubbles. Bring another cup, would you?

He goes into the bedroom.

MARK. The second this Colonel Wilberforce falls in a stupor, bundle him into a taxi—and let me know—

WILLIAMS. Yes, my Lord.

NORA *comes in.*

NORA. Darling, really—you *are* too naughty. They're all screaming for you downstairs.

MARK. I can't come down just yet, darling. I really can't. But, with Williams' help, I have the highest hopes of being down in a very few minutes now—All right, Williams. Thank you. (*He nods to* WILLIAMS, *who goes out.*)

NORA. Well, don't leave it too long, darling, or they'll all begin to believe Mark Wright doesn't exist.

MARK. Mark Wright does exist. In fact Mark Wright has just made a very momentous decision.

NORA. No La Paz?

MARK. No La Paz.

NORA. Thank you. I can't say more. Just thank you. I must go back. Darling there's someone actually aching to meet you. I was showing him some of your work and he said he recognised it.

MARK. (*Pleased*). Oh. Who was that?

NORA. I can't remember his name. Viscount someone or other. He came with Ursula Culpepper. I'll send him up.

MARK. (*Gently*). Darling—two things. First, I told you I didn't want Ursula Culpepper at this party—I detest and deplore the woman——

E

NORA. You can't keep her out, darling. Besides, she *is* my leading lady—after all. I'm so sorry. What's the second thing?

MARK. Well, it's a very tiny little snob point, but you did ask me once to put you right on these things, didn't you?

NORA. Yes, darling——

MARK. Well, one doesn't talk about Viscount so-and-so—one says Lord—(*An appalling thought strikes him. He stops as if shot.*) Viscount who, did you say?

NORA. St—something.

MARK. (*In agony*). With Ursula Culpepper?

NORA. Yes.

MARK. How old?

NORA. Oh. Eighteen—nineteen.

MARK. Yes. I see. (*He looks wildly round the room as if meditating diving through the window.*) Darling—would you think it awfully odd of me if I went out for a little stroll?

NORA. But darling, my party.

MARK. Yes, I know, darling. But sometimes I get the most terrible, terrible claustrophobia at parties.

The words freeze on his lips as DENIS *appears.*

NORA. This is the boy I was telling you about, dear. (*To* DENIS.) Darling, what was that name again?

DENIS. St Neots.

NORA. That's right. Viscount—sorry—Lord St Neots—Mr Wright. I'll leave you two together. (*To* MARK.) Goodbye, my precious. (*She kisses him on the cheek.*) Now don't be too long. I mean it's really too blush-making to give a party just to show off one's gorgeous, glamourous lover, and then he just doesn't put in an appearance at all. (*She goes out. There is an endless pause after she has gone.*)

MARK. (*At length*). These young girls nowadays have a

rather exaggerated way of expressing themselves sometimes.

DENIS. Yes. I know.

MARK. It's what they call being modern, I suppose.

DENIS. I suppose so. (*Pause.*) Very old-fashioned, really
isn't it?

MARK. Yes. I suppose it is. (*Pause.*) You're looking very
brown.

DENIS. I've been sunbathing a lot.

MARK. Yes. Of course. (*Pause.*) Appearances, you know,
Denis, can often be very deceptive.

DENIS. Yes. I know.

MARK. I only say that because I don't want you to jump to
any hasty or rash conclusions.

DENIS. No, Father, I won't.

MARK. I don't know whether you know—as a matter of
fact I don't think you do—that for some time past now I
have been engaged on a little—undercover work for the
Government. I won't tell you any more than that—but
you can probably guess what I'm hinting at.

DENIS. Yes, I think I can.

MARK. Good. Good. Oh, by the way, I'd rather you didn't
give my real name away here if you can avoid it.

DENIS. Of course I won't.

MARK. Miss Patterson and I, of course, are old friends—
very old friends.

DENIS. Yes. I rather gather so—

MARK. But even she doesn't know my real identity—

OSCAR *appears at the bedroom door, on the arm of* BUBBLES.

OSCAR. A nymph! I have found myself a nymph. And
vodka, let me tell you, is the tipple of the world. (*He
comes face to face with the grave-faced* DENIS.) Tiens,
tiens.

DENIS. Hullo, Uncle Oscar.

Pause.

OSCAR. (*Heartily*). Hullo, Denis. You're looking very brown.

MARK. He's been sunbathing.

OSCAR. Oh yes, of course. That would account for it. Well, well, well, well, well. (*After a pause.*) Well, well, well.

BUBBLES. (*To* OSCAR). My God, darling—stop saying "well", it's too shamingly repetitious, and go on with that lovely tickling thing you were doing to the back of my neck——

OSCAR. Er—Miss Fairweather—I wonder if you'd mind awfully going back to bed for a moment. (*He pushes her towards the door.*)

BUBBLES. Well, give me my vodka—(*she takes it, and kisses him on the cheek.*) Baby's not going to be left entirely on her own. (*At the door.*) I'll be waiting, you gorgeous beast. I'll be waiting—(*She goes out.*)

OSCAR. Extraordinary the high spirits of these youngsters, isn't it?

MARK. Yes, it is, isn't it?

OSCAR. Extraordinary. (*Heartily again.*) Well, Denis— quite a surprise bumping into you like this.

DENIS. Yes, I know.

OSCAR. (*Carefully*). Your father's probably told you about how I happened to see him at the Club, and how I said I wanted him to come along to a party that a chap called Wright was giving, because I thought it might amuse him, you know, and of course this girl Nora Patterson is quite an old friend of mine—and your father hadn't even met her, so I thought—(*He stops, noticing the expression on* MARK's *face.*) Isn't that what he told you?

DENIS. No. Not exactly.

OSCAR. (*Aggrieved*). Well, I can't for the life of me think why not.

MARK. Your Uncle Oscar isn't quite accountable for his

actions at the moment, you know, Denis. He had a silly
accident with a cocktail he was mixing, and put brandy
in instead of vermouth. Imagine.

DENIS. Horrible, I should think. And then, of course, with
vodka on top—Look, Father—I'm awfully sorry about
this. I hope you don't think I've done it on purpose or
anything—but I was downstairs and Miss Patterson was
showing me some sculpture and, of course, I recognised
some of it, so I thought I'd better meet this chap Wright,
because I thought perhaps some blighter was pinching
your work or something.

MARK. That's all right, my dear boy. That's perfectly all
right. I quite understand.

DENIS. Of course it was idiotic of me, because I should
have realised the situation at once.

MARK. Oh? Why should you?

DENIS. Well, as soon as I saw Miss Patterson——

MARK. I don't quite follow.

DENIS. Well, of course, she's the living image of Sylvia,
isn't she?

MARK. Sylvia?

DENIS. That face you're always sculpting. The one you
were in love with when you were seventeen——

MARK. Oh. How did you know that?

DENIS. You told me about her.

MARK. I never told you I was in love with her——

DENIS. Oh well, father, that was easy to guess, wasn't it?

MARK. Was it? I didn't know.

DENIS. It's funny, you know. I imagine an awful lot of
people go through life in love with the same face.

MARK. Yes. I imagine they do.

DENIS. It's arrested development, really, isn't it?

MARK. Is it?

DENIS. A sort of narcissism, I think.

MARK. Narcissism?

DENIS. Well, you know—what you're really in love with is your vanished youth. (OSCAR *makes a slight sound.*)

MARK. (*Savagely to* OSCAR). Did you say anything?

OSCAR. No, no. Just a sneeze—that's all.

DENIS. You see, it's really yourself at seventeen that you love.

MARK. Do I?

DENIS. Yes. (*Smiling cheerfully.*) Oh, it's nothing at all to worry about, Father.

MARK. I'm delighted to hear it.

DENIS. I mean—you don't need to go to a psycho-analyst or anything.

MARK. That's good. Psycho-analysts are so expensive, aren't they?

DENIS. Well, as a matter of fact, Father, I do happen to know a very good one in Wigmore Street who'd do you at a reduced rate—if you really wanted to go, that's to say—But I honestly don't think it's necessary. I mean arrested development's awfully common, really. Practically everyone has it, in one form or another——

MARK. Uncle Oscar, for instance?

DENIS. Oh yes. Of course, That's terribly obvious, isn't it?

OSCAR. Is it?

DENIS. Tickling girls on the back of the neck, and all that. It's really children's games, isn't it—I mean, from a strictly Freudian point.

Pause.

OSCAR. Tell me, Denis. What is the address of this man in Wigmore Street?

DENIS. I haven't got it on me. But I'm sure there's nothing to worry about, Father. This looking for Sylvia is really quite harmless. Quite harmless. Well, now, look. I know you'd rather I didn't stay, and I'd like to leave if I could—because I've promised to take Ursula to dinner—

MARK. You mean Ursula Culpepper?

DENIS. Yes.

There is a pause. Then MARK *gathers himself for assault.*

MARK. Ah! Now I thought I had expressly forbidden you ever to see that woman again?

OSCAR. (*Murmuring*). My front is being pierced, my flanks are being turned, I attack. Marshal Foch.

MARK. (*After glaring at* OSCAR.) Is that, or is that not so, Denis?

DENIS. Yes, Father. But I never promised and I'm afraid I didn't accept your judgment in this case.

MARK. Oh? You didn't? Well, you'd better accept it now. I won't have my son consorting with one of the most notorious women in London.

DENIS. She can't help being notorious, Father. She's such a famous actress. Wonderful actress, too. Have you ever seen her?

MARK. No. I am happy to say, not.

DENIS. I'm surprised. She's starring in the same play that Miss Patterson is a super in——

Pause.

OSCAR. Of course that flank was badly exposed—invited counter-attack——

MARK. (*After another glance at* OSCAR). A woman with the mind and the vocabulary of a streetwalker——

DENIS. Yes, I know, Father. It's awfully boring, that outspokenness. I often tell her so. It's what we were saying a moment ago about Miss Patterson, isn't it?

OSCAR. Oh dear. Clean through the centre now.

MARK. Oscar, I trust I shall not have to ask you to leave the room.

OSCAR. I'm sorry. It's the vodka——

MARK (*To* DENIS). Leaving the subject of Ursula Culpepper for the moment only—Denis—may I ask you for an explanation of your extraordinary conduct in leaving Tours at a moment's notice, and flying to London?

DENIS. I'm sorry, Father, but I couldn't stick it there another second. After all I'd been there three months—

MARK. And how much French have you learnt in those three months may I ask? Dites-moi quelque chose en français——

DENIS. Que voulez-vous que je vous dis?

MARK. (*Triumphantly*). Dise. Que je vous dise. Subjunctive. And your accent is abominable.

OSCAR. Ah. An advance. A minor one—perhaps—but still an advance——

MARK. (*Furiously*). Oscar—will you keep quiet?

DENIS. Anyway, Father, there's no real point in my learning French, is there, because I've decided to become an actor.

MARK. Oh you have, have you? You've decided to become an actor?

NORA *comes in*.

NORA. Darling, I'm just going to put on that new hat you gave me, to show Babs. (*She crosses to the bedroom door*.) What *is* going on up here?

MARK. Nothing, my dear. Nothing.

NORA. Darling, if you don't come down in a minute I think I'll get cross. Except that I couldn't really get cross with you, today, could I, after your being such a sweetie and giving up that horrid, horrid La Paz for me——

MARK. Yes, well, we'll talk about all that later. (*She goes into the bedroom*.)

DENIS. (*reproachfully*). Oh, Father! You're not giving up the Diplomatic, are you?

Pause.

OSCAR. (*To* MARK). I think, my dear chap—there's nothing for it but to prepare for an eventual evacuation——

MARK. Oscar. Leave the room.

OSCAR. I was on the point of doing so. The whole scene is far too painful for me.

COLONEL WILBERFORCE's *jovial head appears at the door.*
OSCAR *flies to a corner of the room and examines a picture.*

WILBERFORCE. Ah, Binfield. So that's where you've been hiding yourself is it? Can't say I blame you. Terrible party, isn't it?

MARK. You're not enjoying it, Colonel?

WILBERFORCE. Hating it, my dear fellow. Positively hating it. Of course, I'd never have come if it hadn't been for my wife. She was on the stage you know. (*Seeing* DENIS.) Oh, isn't this your boy?

MARK. Yes.

WILBERFORCE. I thought so. Saw you bat at Lord's, young fellow. Shouldn't have got out that way. Shocking stroke. Yes, my wife was in that show *Topsy Turvy*. Expect you saw it. She was the one who came out at the end and said, "So you were really Lord Percy all along?" Do you remember?

MARK. Yes, of course.

WILBERFORCE. Good. You heard her all right, did you?

MARK. As clear as a bell.

WILBERFORCE. I only ask because some friends of mine said they had difficulty in catching the words. Of course I couldn't really judge because, you see, I knew the part.

MARK. No. I see. Exactly——

OSCAR *is examining the picture with great apparent interest.*
WILBERFORCE *looks at him with faint suspicion.*

WILBERFORCE. Tell me, does anyone here know a terrible bounder by the name of Philipson?

He says it to OSCAR *who shakes his head vaguely.*

I hear he's at this party. I'm extremely anxious to have a word with the blighter——

After a pregnant pause DENIS *steps forward.*

DENIS. Er—may I introduce—Brigadier Mason—er— Colonel——

WILBERFORCE. Wilberforce. How do you do? You're very young to be a Brigadier.

OSCAR. So many people tell me——

There is the sound of a woman singing raucously, loudly and drunkenly in the street.

WILBERFORCE. Oh. Excuse me a second. I think that's my wife—(*Crossing to window.*) Yes, it is. Astonishing thing. Never drinks at all you know. All she ever does at a party is to take an occasional sip from my glass.

MARK. Indeed, Colonel? Is that all she ever does? Just take an occasional sip from your glass?

WILBERFORCE. Yes. That's all. Can't understand it at all— (*Out of window to his invisible wife.*) Hullo, darling. Yoo Hoo! (*A woman's voice is heard in response.*) Look—you —there—Williams, isn't it?

WILLIAMS. (*Off*). O.K. sir.

WILBERFORCE. Now just you get hold of her. (*Her voice is heard in protest.*) Don't let go of her, man. Get her into that taxi. (*There is the noise of a taxi door slamming, then silence.*) Safely stowed, as they say in the play. Williams did it on his own—capital fellow, that. Goodbye, young feller. Keep a straighter bat next time. Goodbye, Brigadier. Goodbye, Binfield. Nice seeing you again.

NORA *emerges from the bedroom.*

WILBERFORCE. Ah, our hostess. Just saying goodbye—

NORA. Oh. Are you leaving so soon?

WILBERFORCE. Yes. Slight accident to Betty. Can't fathom it. Can't fathom it at all. Goodbye. Charming party. Afraid I never had a chance to meet our host. Say goodbye to him for me, would you?

NORA. (*indicating* MARK). Well, you can do it yourself, can't you?

WILBERFORCE. What? Binfield? Binfield the host? That's good, isn't it, old chap? Well, goodbye, everyone. Oh, Binfield, congratulations on being made Minister in La

Paz, by the way. Splendid appointment. Splendid. Goodbye. (*He goes, leaving a heavy silence behind him.*)

NORA. Darling, you'll forgive me for being inquisitive, won't you?

There is a pause. Then MARK *clears his throat resignedly.*

MARK. Nora. I realise perfectly that what I am going to tell you may seem not unlike the plot of *Topsy-Turvy*, but I must inform you that I am not Mr Wright, but Lord Binfield; and that this is my son, Denis.

NORA. (*Seizing the salient point*). Your son? (*She looks at* DENIS *and then at* MARK.) Oh, darling. I mean you couldn't have really—could you?

MARK. No. My age, too, I have lied about. I am not thirty-five, but forty-four.

NORA. Darling! Three one can forgive. Nine is really going too far. Well, it's all too wildly exciting and improbable —just like *life*, my darlings—but we really haven't time to discuss it all now. I'm going back to the party. (*She goes to the door.*) Oh, by the way—in case anybody's even remotely interested—I am actually the rightful Princess Amalia of Bottleburg and Bubbles Fairweather is my mother—the Grand Duchess——

She goes out. There is a long pause.

OSCAR. (*At length*). Tiens, tiens.

MARK *sits heavily, and rests his head in his hands.*

OSCAR. (*Again*). Tiens, tiens.

DENIS *goes up to* MARK'S *chair.* MARK *looks up at him, glaring.*

DENIS. Father, may I say something? (MARK *looks at him in silence.*) I know it's none of my business—but really, you know, I do think you're making rather a mistake chucking the Diplomatic. (*Very sincerely.*) I know exactly how you feel and I do sympathise with you—really I do. But you've had such a brilliant career up to now— haven't you—I do think it'd be an awful waste to throw it all away now. (MARK *still makes no reply. He seems rather moved.*) . . . Could we have dinner together, father?

MARK. I understood you were dining with Ursula Culpepper.

DENIS. That's all right. I'll put her off. She won't mind. Do come, Father.

MARK. I've got an engagement too.

DENIS. Couldn't you chuck it? I tell you what—let's dine at my club. The food's not up to much, but we can talk there and not be disturbed. I'll just dash down and explain to Ursula. You will come, won't you?

There is a pause.

MARK. I don't know, Denis. I don't know. I think probably not.

DENIS. (*Cheerfully*). Well, I'll put Ursula off, anyway. Won't be a second. (DENIS *goes out.*)

OSCAR, *who has watched the preceding scene without stirring, looks at* MARK. MARK *answers the look. Then he deliberately gets up and goes into the hall, reappearing in a second with hat, gloves and an overcoat.* OSCAR *helps him on with his overcoat—still in silence. He starts slowly for the hall.*

OSCAR. Mark?

MARK. Yes, Oscar?

OSCAR. What a loss to the Diplomatic that boy is going to be.

MARK. Loss? (*It has taken him a second to see what* OSCAR *means.*) Now let me tell you, Oscar—if Denis thinks for one moment I am going to countenance——

DENIS *reappears.*

DENIS. I've got a taxi, Father——

MARK. (*Turning on him angrily*). You realise, Denis, that this is not going to be a very pleasant dinner for you— don't you? I'm going to have a few very strong words to say to you tonight——

DENIS. Yes, Father.

MARK. An actor, indeed! What in the name of heaven makes you think you can be an actor?

DENIS. Oh. I don't know, Father. I just do. That's all.

MARK. Have you by any chance forgotten that one day you're going to inherit my name?

DENIS. Well, I could always have a stage name, couldn't I, Father? I mean, after all, I suppose I could call myself Denis Wright.

Pause. OSCAR *throws his hands in the air.*

OSCAR. Complete break-through! Utter collapse along the entire front! Sue for terms, Mark—sue for terms.

MARK *advances on him belligerently.*

MARK. My God! Somctimes I feel like knocking you through a window.

OSCAR. All right. Why don't you?

MARK. (*His voice strangled with fury*). Because—Oh, because you're so bloody fat. (*He turns abruptly on* DENIS.) Now listen, Denis, if you think for one minute that you've got the faintest chance in the world of getting away with this arrant folly—you're making the biggest mistake of your young life——

As they reach the hall, the CURTAIN has fallen.

ACT III

SCENE: *The same.   Time: 1950.*

The room once more has had a change of character, and has reverted rather to its original bachelor quality—though it gives the impression, here and there, of having tried hard to make itself look like a love nest—(1950 version) and of having failed to carry out its purpose through being too well-bred.

It is about 6.30 of a winter evening and on the rise of the curtain, WILLIAMS *is discovered on the telephone. The dinner table is laid for four places. The meal is evidently to be of oysters only, and champagne. The radio can now be distinguished as playing the "Harry Lime Theme".*

WILLIAMS (*into telephone*). Sloane 7838? Cunliffe there? Oh, hullo, cock . . . It's me. Here's the yarn for tonight. Got a pencil? . . . yes, you'll need it . . . Ready. (*Dictating slowly.*) I'm the hall porter at the club . . . Yes . . . He's dining here—that's to say at the club—with General Philipson . . . Yes, that's easy, it's what comes later . . . Got that? O.K. . . . Dining at the club with the General, going straight to Mr Denis's first night, where he's meeting Lord Bayswater and the Minister for War . . . War . . . After the theatre going to Lord Bayswater's for supper. Expect to be home about 12.30 . . . O.K. . . . Say one, it's safer . . . Tell me, how's her Ladyship's cold? Better? . . . Oh, good . . . got up this afternoon. Yes, I'll tell him. He'll be pleased. O.K. Now have you got that straight? O.K. chum, that's it . . . O.K. Be seeing you. (*He rings off.*)

DORIS *and* CHLOE *come in together, talking.* DORIS *is putting a latchkey away in her bag. Both girls are exquisitely dressed*

*in evening gowns, and carry themselves like mannequins,
which indeed they are.* DORIS *is the* 1950 *edition of* SYLVIA.
CHLOE *is very beautiful and very statuesque.*

DORIS. So I said to Madam, I said, personally I never have
thought an hour was enough at lunch time and just because
I'm ten minutes late it doesn't mean the whole dressmaking
business is going to go bankrupt, does it? (*To* WILLIAMS)
Good evening, dear. This is Chloe—Mr Williams.
She's at Fabia's too——

WILLIAMS (*to* CHLOE). How do you do, Miss?

CHLOE. Good evening.

DORIS. Came along at a moment's notice—very kind of her
I do think, just to make up the party, and she had a date
with a gentleman, too——

CHLOE. No. With my Mum.

DORIS. Oh, with your Mum, was it dear? How nice. (*To*
WILLIAMS.) Neither of us have had a minute to do a
thing to ourselves, as you know, dear, with Mr Wright
ringing up like that at the last second. I'm sure we look
positive frights——

WILLIAMS. Oh no, Miss. You look as gorgeous as ever, and
the other lady a fair treat, if I may say so. Pleasure to
look at you both, I must say——

DORIS. Oh, but we just literally threw ourselves into our
clothes, didn't we, dear?

CHLOE. Oh yes, dear. Just bundled ourselves in any old
how—shocking it was.

DORIS, *as she speaks, is crossing the room with the slow,
assured walk of the girl who is exquisitely dressed and
knows it, and* CHLOE *as she speaks sits down with all the
grace and dignity of a princess.*

DORIS (*inspecting the table*). Oysters. Do you like oysters,
dear?

CHLOE. Not very much, dear. Do you?

WILLIAMS (*to* CHLOE). Well, I'm very sorry, Miss, but I'm

afraid that's all there is. Just a little *bonne bouche* before the theatre, as you might say. You'll be having supper afterwards, of course——

CHLOE (*languidly*). Oh well, of course—if that's all there is——

DORIS. What's that book you're reading, dear?

WILLIAMS. Trevelyan's *Social History*, Miss.

DORIS. Why ever do you read that?

WILLIAMS. I find it very enjoyable, and most illuminating. Well, I must be off. Going to see Mr Denis, too. This Old Vic's a shocking place to get to.

DORIS. And who are you taking to the play?

WILLIAMS. Oh, no one, Miss. You know me——

DORIS. You don't like ladies much, do you dear?

WILLIAMS. I'm too old for ladies now, Miss. I used to like 'em once—in their place, of course.

DORIS. Oh. And what do you think is their place?

WILLIAMS *for reply, merely smiles.*

WILLIAMS. Well. Goodnight, ladies. Be good. (*He goes.*)

CHLOE (*languidly*). What's the show we're going to see?

DORIS. It's *Julius Cæsar*, I think, dear. You know—Shakespeare.

CHLOE (*her face fallen*). Shakespeare? You didn't say that——

DORIS. Didn't I? Oh well, I expect it'll be quite good. It often *is* quite good, you know, Shakespeare. It's quite a surprise, sometimes.

CHLOE. I didn't like the other one—that one Mr Wetherby took us to——

DORIS. That wasn't Shakespeare, dear. It was quite modern, Mr. Wetherby was saying. He said the man who wrote it is still alive. Fancy.

CHLOE. Of course it wasn't modern, silly. It was poetical. And they were all dressed up mediaeval——

DORIS. A play can be poetical and dressed up mediaeval

and still be modern, dear, if it's by a man who's still
alive.

CHLOE. Well, I didn't understand it anyway.

DORIS (*patiently*). Nor did I, dear. Not a bloody word. But
that still doesn't make it Shakespeare, dear, does it——

CHLOE (*giving up*). Well, you might have told me it was
Shakespeare tonight—I do think.

DORIS. I know *you*, dear. You'd have cried off. I told you it
was Denis Wright——

CHLOE. Yes, but in *Julius Cæsar*. (*A horrifying thought
strikes her.*) Why, that's B.C.——

DORIS. I don't know why you always mind B.C. so much,
dear. I think B.C.'s quite pleasant, sometimes. Makes a
nice change——

CHLOE. What part will Denis Wright be? Julius Cæsar?

DORIS. No—I expect he'll be the one that says "Friends,
Romans, Countrymen——"

CHLOE (*brightening a little*). Oh, is that in it? I know that.
I'll look out for that. Mr Wright is Denis Wright's
father, you said——

DORIS. That's it, dear. Mr Mark Wright. As a matter of
fact he's Lord Binfield—really——

CHLOE. Oh!

DORIS. The British Ambassador in Paris.

CHLOE. Fancy!

DORIS. Don't let on you know, dear, will you—because the
old chap does so like us all to think he's just Mr
Wright——

CHLOE. Why?

DORIS. I don't know, really. I think quite a lot of gentlemen
are rather like that. They'd think it terribly immoral to
deceive their wives under their own names. Take
another, and they'll be up to Lord knows what, and as
gay and as innocent as sandboys——

CHLOE. Yes—but being an Earl and an Ambassador and all

F

that, you'd think he wouldn't have a chance of getting away with another name, would you?

DORIS. Well, of course, dear, he hasn't. The number of times I've had to pretend to be blind, deaf and half-witted, I can't tell you. Still the old boy prefers it that way, and I wouldn't like to spoil his fun.

CHLOE. What's the other one like? This general?

DORIS. Oh, he's quite a nice old thing in his way. Quite harmless really. Oh, by the way, he likes to be known as Major Mason——

CHLOE. Why *Major*?

DORIS. He thinks it makes him sound younger. Sweet, isn't it?

CHLOE (*gloomily*). I don't think old gentlemen are ever sweet. I don't think I like old gentlemen at all.

DORIS. Old gentlemen are much nicer than young ones, they've got such lovely manners for one thing. I mean with an old gentleman, for instance, a headache's a headache and no nonsense. My dear, I'm forgetting *my* manners now. Would you care to powder your nose?

CHLOE. Yes, I think that might be a good idea.

DORIS. This way, then, dear. (*She sweeps majestically to the bedroom door, and holds it open for* CHLOE.)

CHLOE. Oh! What a very nice bedroom!

DORIS. Yes, it is quite nice really, isn't it? I mean when you consider that it's really never used—— This way, dear, on the right. (*She follows* CHLOE *out*.)

After a moment we hear male voices in the hall, and then MARK *and* OSCAR *come in.* MARK *is now 64, and* OSCAR *67. Both have worn quite well. They are in dinner jackets and overcoats. The latter they now proceed to shed.* OSCAR *with a certain amount of coughing and spluttering.*

MARK. My dear chap, you never knew a single word of Shakespeare . . . nothing but a common soldier . . . put your coat down there . . . "*bleeding* piece of earth. Oh pardon me, thou bleeding piece of earth"—not "bloody piece of earth." You never could quote anything correctly.

OSCAR. It's "bloody. Oh pardon me, thou bloody piece of—" (*He stops in a fit of coughing*).

MARK. Nonsense. I say, old chap, that cough of yours is rather worrying, isn't it?

OSCAR. It doesn't worry me, so I don't know why on earth it should worry you——

MARK. Are you sure you oughtn't to keep your coat on?

OSCAR. Quite sure——

MARK. I'll tell you what. I'll find you a rug——

OSCAR. If you think I'm going to dine on oysters and champagne with two girls in a rug, you're off your head——

MARK. Mustn't take needless risks, though. We're none of us quite as young as we were, you know.

OSCAR. What a damned idiotic remark! No, and we're none of us quite as old as we're going to be either.

MARK. It's extraordinary how you get more crotchety and more like a general every day——

OSCAR. And you get more cliché-ridden and more like an ambassador. By the way—kindly remember I'm not a general tonight—I'm a major.

MARK. My dear chap—I don't forget things of that kind. You might be careful about my age too while you're about it.

OSCAR. What is it now?

MARK. Well—you don't need to be too specific. Middle fifties——

OSCAR. Ha!

MARK. You said something?

OSCAR. I said "Ha." What's young Denis going to be like?

MARK (*ponderously*). Well—now, Oscar—you know that I am not in any way prone to exaggeration——

OSCAR. Do I?

MARK (*ignoring him*). And you know too that I have never been in any shape or form prejudiced by the mere fact that Denis happens to be my son.

OSCAR. Do I?

MARK. Nevertheless I am not, I think, making any ill-considered statement when I say that Denis's Mark Antony—without the slightest question—is the greatest I have seen since Irving.

OSCAR. You didn't see Irving.

MARK. How do you know I didn't?

OSCAR. Because he didn't play it.

MARK. Well, then, you didn't either, so shut up.

OSCAR (*a shade timorously*). What exactly are the plans for later?

MARK. Doris and I will be having a little supper here. I assumed you would be making rather similar arrangements.

OSCAR. Well, I've laid on a tentative little cold collation for two in my rooms.

MARK. Why tentative? Have you lost your nerve?

OSCAR (*sadly*). No. Just my youth.

MARK. Nonsense. Never say die is my motto.

OSCAR. We may not say it, old chap—but quite soon we'll have to do it.

MARK. Certainly. And, speaking for myself, when I do do it, I'll look back on an exceptionally well-ordered and well-conducted life. Or rather lives.

OSCAR. It beats me how you've got away with both of them all these years.

MARK. Well. It doesn't beat me. I've got away with them for precisely the reasons I've always told you I would get away with them. Skill, application, finesse, and a superb talent for organisation. You know, Oscar, I may well have stumbled on the whole secret of successful living.

OSCAR. Hmm!

MARK. To divide the illicit from the domestic, the romantic
and dangerous from the dull and secure—to divide them
into two worlds and then to have the best of both of
them. Years ago in this very room you told me it
couldn't be done—Well, I've done it—not only here in
London, but in Paris, in Rome, in Stockholm, and in La
Paz.

OSCAR. What are you in Paris? Monsieur Droit, l'espion-
extraordinaire?

MARK. No. Just Mr Wright, the English sculptor. A
fourth floor studio in Montparnasse. A little model——

OSCAR. Called Mimi.

MARK. Albertine.

OSCAR. Dying of consumption?

MARK. No. Just an existentialist. Mr Wright is very
happy in Paris. And so, may I add, is Lord Binfield.

OSCAR. Luck! That's all it's been from the beginning. Luck
and nothing else.

MARK. I don't recognise the term.

OSCAR. But, my God—you take such appalling risks. Look
at tonight, for instance——

MARK. Tonight? Tonight is an excellent example of my
aptitude for planning. At the last minute I learn that my
wife has influenza, and that the doctor has forbidden her
to go out. What do I do? Quick as thought I ring up
Charlie Bayswater, who I know is going to the theatre
with his friend the War Minister, and make a date with
him for five minutes before curtain up in the bar, where
all the photographers will be floating around. Too good
a catch to miss—the four of us. (*Triumphantly.*) In the
Tatler to show my wife on Wednesday——

OSCAR. And the girls?

MARK. The girls have their explicit instructions. You and
I, on leaving the bar and the photographers, will pro-

ceed to our seats—and there sitting right next to us will be the two ladies whom we happened to have met at the Dutch Embassy last Monday. Fancy that. The operation of having one's cake and eating it is so absurdly simple, if performed with the necessary attention to detail and organisation. (*The telephone rings. He gets up to answer it.*) (*Into telephone.*) Hullo . . . Hullo? . . . Who? (*His face shows acute alarm. In a badly disguised voice.*) Oh no, 'e's not 'ere. What nime shall I tell 'im . . . Yes. milady . . . Very good, milady . . . No, the General's not 'ere, neither . . . No, milady . . . No, I don't know, milady . . . (*He rings off. In a whisper.*) How in the name of heaven did she know this number?

OSCAR. The missus? (MARK *nods distractedly.*)

MARK. Yes, she must still have your number in her book.

OSCAR. But dammit, she knows I haven't lived here for donkey's years. Anyway, the number's been changed.

MARK. Perhaps she's delirious——

OSCAR. Did she sound delirious?

MARK. No. But they never do. Do you think I ought to go back?

OSCAR. Why don't you ring up?

MARK. Yes. I will. Good gracious. The girls! (*He is on his way to the telephone when the bedroom door opens and the two* GIRLS *come out.*)

DORIS (*as she enters*)—it's got the plunging neckline, but of course it's strictly 1950—oh, hullo. You been here long, dear?

MARK. We didn't realise you were gossiping in there——

DORIS. My dear, you'd only got to shout out. Oh, Chloe, I don't think you've met Mr Wright, have you?

MARK. How do you do?

CHLOE. How do you do? Very honoured, I'm sure, to meet Denis Wright's father——

MARK. Once upon a time, you know, Denis Wright was known as my son. Now I'm known as his father—it's rather shaming, isn't it?

CHLOE. Shaming? What a quaint, old-fashioned word. I rather like it, don't you, Doris? Shaming?

DORIS. Yes, dear. This is General—er—Major Mason, dear. Do you remember I told you all about him——

OSCAR (*winningly*). Oh—not *all* about me, I hope. (*He laughs seductively, but it lapses into a wheezy cough.*)

MARK. The Major's got a slight cold, I'm afraid. Caught it out duck-shooting—didn't you, Major?

OSCAR. Yes. Gets a bit chilly, you know, out there in the marshes. Many chaps younger than myself go down with pneumonia, you know——

CHLOE. Well, it seems rather silly to do it then, doesn't it?

OSCAR. Ah, but then a cold is a small sacrifice to pay for the pleasures of an active life, don't you think?

CHLOE. No. I don't think I do. And I do hope you're not going to go giving your cold to me——

OSCAR. If you would allow me but the faintest chance of giving you anything, dear young lady, even my cold, I would count myself amongst the happiest of mortals——

MARK. Well now—shall we sit down?

DORIS (*sitting*). Come on, Chloe.

MARK. Come along, Major, lend a hand.

OSCAR. Yes, it would indeed be a pleasure to act as your Ganymede, dear lady.

CHLOE (*to* DORIS *in an undertone as she sits*). He talks so high-flown.

DORIS. They all do, dear. It's nice.

CHLOE. I don't think so. I think it's sort of—well—in-decent.

OSCAR (*to* MARK). Well, why don't you slip out and ring her up?

MARK (*to* OSCAR, *in an undertone*). I'll ring up from the

theatre. Well, now, oysters. Doris and Chloe, if I may take that liberty——

CHLOE (*to* DORIS). What liberty?

DORIS (*in an undertone*). Saying Chloe, dear.

CHLOE. What's a liberty about that?

DORIS. Sh!

OSCAR *takes the vacant seat, coughing a little as he does so.*

MARK. Sure I can't get you a little covering for your shoulders, Major?

OSCAR. No thank you, Wright. I wouldn't like the ladies to think I'm Whistler's mother. (DORIS *laughs gaily.*)

DORIS. Oh, that's good, Major. That's very good. Whistler's mother! Isn't that good, Chloe?

CHLOE (*mistiming it badly*). Yes. (*She laughs tinnily.*) Very good. Go on about what you said to Madam, dear.

MARK *meanwhile, has opened the champagne, while* OSCAR *sits, a neglected and forlorn figure, between the two girls.*

DORIS. Well—I said—after all ten minutes isn't very much when you think that Princess Kasbak is a good half-hour late every day and Madam never says anything to her.

CHLOE. Do you know what I think Madam is?—A snob. That's what Madam is. Anyway, she's not a Princess— not a real one.

DORIS. Well, I don't know dear, she does come from Anatolia.

CHLOE. I come from Pinner, but it doesn't make me a Countess. Besides, if she was a real princess she'd be at Hartnell's. (*Examining the champagne bottle as* MARK *pours.*) Oh, it isn't Bollinger?

MARK. No. It's Moet and Chandon '37. Would you rather have had Bollinger?

CHLOE. Oh well—it doesn't really matter now you've poured. (MARK *passes on to* DORIS, OSCAR *and himself.*) (*To* DORIS.) Yes, dear, I quite agree. Madam really is the

limit. I mean, look at the way she treats Mr. Claud—
and of course, Madam and Mr. Freddy, well, I mean, we
all know, don't we? And then again, dear, I've seen
Madam sometimes——

MARK (*sitting and raising his glass*). Well, ladies, I'll just
say, Here's to love!

DORIS ⎱ (*murmuring*). To love. (*They take a very per-*
CHLOE ⎰   *functory sip.*)

CHLOE (*to* DORIS)——I mean, I've seen Madam simply
furious with Mr Claud for no reason at all.

DORIS. Yes, dear. And what about that time when she made
such a scene over that gold lamé?

CHLOE. Wasn't it a scream? (*Both girls laugh gaily.*)

DORIS (*imitating Madam, apparently*). Pull those sleeves off!
Pull those sleeves off, this instant!

CHLOE (*imitating Mr. Claud, apparently*). Madam—you're
breaking my heart. You're breaking my heart! Let go,
Madam. Let go! (*They laugh again.* OSCAR *talks to* MARK
across the table. As they converse, the GIRLS *are continuing
their own discussion.*)

OSCAR. Do you get much golf these days?

MARK. No. Not much. An occasional round at St. Cloud.

OSCAR. St. Cloud? Yes, I've played there. It's quite a good
course, isn't it?

MARK. Not bad. It plays rather short though——

OSCAR. I remember the ninth, I think. Isn't that the hole
with the trees behind the green, and an enormous
bunker on the right?

MARK. No. I think that's the eleventh you're thinking
of——

OSCAR. Oh, the eleventh, is it? I thought it was the ninth.
(*Simultaneously,* DORIS *and* CHLOE.)

DORIS. Oh, it was a shame really, because it wasn't so bad
that dress. Do you remember it, dear, with that shaped
bodice and the crinoline?

CHLOE. Oh yes, dear, I remember it very well. I thought it was quite unreasonable of Madam to go on like that——

DORIS. Well, of course, that's the trouble with Madam. I mean, she *is* unreasonable. I mean, look what she said to Gladys yesterday.

CHLOE. Oh, I didn't hear about that. What did she say?

DORIS. Oh, it was terrible. She said "Get out," she said, "get out—you're nothing but a . . ." (*She lowers her voice to a whisper, happily inaudible to all but* CHLOE. *The* MEN *have concluded their golfing conversation.*)

CHLOE. She didn't!

DORIS. She did. (*She repeats the three words, of which we can now tell that the middle one is "little" and the last monosyllabic, necessitating a rounding of the lips. The first might be anything beginning with B.*)

CHLOE. Oh—how dreadful.

DORIS. Unreasonable, you see. Just unreasonable. (*She makes a face at* CHLOE, *significant of unreasonableness and then becomes conscious of her social duties. To* MARK.) Well, dear. How are you?

MARK. Oh, I'm very well, thank you, Doris.

DORIS. That's good.

MARK. And how are you?

DORIS. Oh, so so, you know. I've got this headache again——

MARK (*gloomily*). Oh no! (*Pause.*)

CHLOE. Funny—your saying that, Doris, because I've got an absolutely splitting headache.

DORIS. Oh, you poor thing! I am sorry.

OSCAR (*to* CHLOE). Where exactly is your headache, dear lady? Here? (*He touches her forehead.*)

CHLOE. Well—all over, really——

OSCAR. All over? Ah then, I've got exactly the thing for it. The very latest drug. I believe Mark and Doris are deserting us after the play, so if you would do me the honour of having a little supper with me at my flat, I could give it to you, then.

CHLOE. Oh. (*Faintly.*) How nice! (*She makes a despairing face at* DORIS *across the table.*)

MARK (*at the window*). The car is there.

OSCAR (*looking at his watch*). We've got plenty of time. We've got well over half an hour.

MARK. I like to be early. Shall we leave the ladies, Major?

OSCAR *gets up, fails to make it first time, and sits down again.*

OSCAR. Funny thing—my knee caught the leg of the table. (*He laughs jovially, the laugh once more becoming a cough.* MARK *comes to help him.*)

MARK. Let me give you a hand.

OSCAR (*testily*). All right, all right. I can manage. (*He strikes out vigorously for the bedroom door.*) From the way he treats me sometimes, you'd think I was an old cripple, or something. (*He laughs gaily, waves to the ladies, disappears and we hear a crash as he enters the bedroom.*)

MARK (*alarmed*). Good heavens! Major! What have you done? (MARK *follows him into the bedroom.*)

DORIS. You see, dear, what I say about old gentlemen is that they're so cosy. Cosy old ducks—that's what they are——

CHLOE (*plainly miserable*). Well, I don't think my one's cosy at all.

DORIS. Oh, he's really quite a dear, the General, when you get to know him.

CHLOE. I don't think I want to get to know him.

DORIS. You mustn't mind just because he talks high-flown, dear. I was telling you, they all talk high-flown——

CHLOE (*imitating*). If I might have the honour—dear lady —a little supper at my flat—I would count myself the happiest of mortals—I mean, it's practically Lord Byron, isn't it?

DORIS. Well, I think that's nice, dear, don't you?

CHLOE. No. I think I want to go home.

DORIS. Oh, what a shame!

CHLOE. I shouldn't really have come out at all. I promised Mum I'd help her with the washing—and I could have got on with that jumper——

DORIS. Well, all right, dear, you go off. They won't mind. That's what's so nice about old gentlemen. They never mind anything—— (*The sound of the old gentlemen's voices can be heard approaching the bedroom door.*) Here they are. Don't you say anything, dear. I'll fix it. (MARK *and* OSCAR *come in.*)

MARK (*as he enters*)—but why ring up here, anyway? She thinks I'm at my club. And how on earth could she possibly know the number——

OSCAR. Don't ask me, old chap.

MARK. Well, well. All ready?

DORIS. Oh dear—isn't it a shame? Chloe's been taken quite queer, quite suddenly.

MARK. Oh. I'm so sorry.

DORIS. She thinks it must have been a bad oyster, don't you, dear?

CHLOE. Yes. That's right, dear. A bad oyster.

MARK. It couldn't have been a bad oyster. These oysters came from my club——

DORIS. Poor Chloe! She feels she ought to go straight home, don't you, dear?

OSCAR. Oh, no.

CHLOE. Oh, yes. I must go home. Otherwise I might break out in a rash in the stalls, and that'd be terrible wouldn't it?

DORIS. I'll drive her home, dear. Won't take me five minutes——

OSCAR. Look—let me drive her home.

CHLOE (*sharply*). Oh, no. (*Recovering herself.*) Oh, no, Major, please don't bother.

OSCAR (*winningly*). My dear young lady, I can assure you that the inestimable boon of prolonging our all too brief acquaintance by an extra five minutes would far outweigh the faintest element of bother—— (CHLOE *stares at him, as if he were some particularly repulsive cobra, momentarily in the guise of Lord Byron. She gives a faint shudder and turns quickly to* MARK.)

CHLOE. Well—it *has* been nice, Mr Wright. Perhaps you'll let me come again some time. Come on, Doris.

OSCAR (*advancing on her*). And how may I give myself the pleasure of a renewal of this encounter?

CHLOE (*helplessly*). Is it my 'phone number you want?

OSCAR. That would be a privilege indeed.

CHLOE. Well—you can always get me at Fabia's, except that Madam doesn't really like us being rung up in working hours—and I can't go upsetting Madam, can I? Because, you see, I'm really only there working hours. Come on, Doris. (SHE *darts out.* DORIS *lingers at the door.*)

DORIS (*To* OSCAR). Don't worry, General. I'll fix things. (SHE *follows* CHLOE *out.* OSCAR *shrugs his shoulders forlornly.*)

MARK (*chuckling*). Poor old Oscar. What very bad luck.

OSCAR. I can't really see what you find so hilarious about having poisoned one of your guests.

MARK (*laughing*). Nonsense. She's not poisoned, she's running away from you, that's all.

OSCAR. There's no need for you to laugh. If I'm a joke, so are you.

MARK. Joke? Speak for yourself.

OSCAR. I'm speaking for both of us. You know what we are, Mark—just a couple of stock Punch figures for whom the austerity age has no further use.

MARK. Nonsense, Oscar. It's got plenty of use. Even the austerity age has to have generals and ambassadors.

OSCAR. Yes—but not my kind of general—nor your kind of ambassador. Austerity generals—austerity ambassadors. My God—you see them around everywhere—drinking dill water and eating grated carrots and talking basic English. Heavens! How I hate austerity, don't you?

MARK. I can't hate it. I represent it. (*There is the noise of a stone against the window.*) What was that?

OSCAR. Stone at the window. (*There is another stone.*) There it is again.

MARK *goes to the window.*

MARK. It's probably Doris. She must have forgotten her key—— (*Looking out.*) Doris?

VOICE. Mark!

MARK (*he hurtles backwards into the room, speechless*). My God! My God! Oscar—My God!

OSCAR. What's the matter?

MARK. Caroline.

OSCAR (*rising*). It couldn't be!

MARK. It is. It is. (*A woman's voice can be heard calling.*)

CAROLINE (*off*). Mark! Mark! Don't be so idiotic. Let me in.

MARK (*in a panic*). She's seen me. I'm lost.

OSCAR. Say it's my flat. We're dining here alone——

MARK. Doris will be back——

CAROLINE (*off*). I'm freezing out here, and I've got a cold anyway. Hurry up, Mark—for pity's sake——

OSCAR. I'll say Doris is my friend. Better let her in, Mark.

MARK (*keening softly*). Oh, my God! Oh, Oscar, how awful! (*He slowly approaches the window. Out of the window, in tones of exaggerated sangfroid.*) Hullo? Who is that? Oh, Caroline. What a surprise! I thought you were in bed.

CAROLINE (*off*). Well, I'm not, my dear. I'm out here. But I'll be in my coffin tomorrow if you don't let me in.

MARK (*with apparent surprise*). Let you in. Oh yes. (*Loudly *to* OSCAR.) Oscar, Oscar, let Caroline into your flat. Just coming, Caroline.

OSCAR. Is she delirious?

MARK. She didn't seem to be——

OSCAR. I mean—she's not in her dressing gown or anything?

MARK. I didn't notice.

OSCAR. You must have noticed.

MARK. Go and let her in, Oscar.

OSCAR *goes out.* MARK, *left alone, rushes to try to remove traces of the two girls' presence. He is in the act of bundling plates into a drawer when the front door is heard opening.* CAROLINE *comes in, followed by* OSCAR. *She is an imposing old lady of decided beauty, dressed in an evening gown and a cloak.*)

CAROLINE. Good evening, dear.

MARK. Good evening, Caroline. Oughtn't you to be in bed?

CAROLINE. I got up this afternoon because I had no temperature. I took it again at five and I still hadn't one, so I decided to come to the first night. You've given my seat to Charlie Bayswater, haven't you, dear?

MARK. Oh, yes, but he's chucked.

CAROLINE. How fortunate.

MARK. Very lucky you finding me here, Caroline—in Oscar's flat.

CAROLINE. Yes, dear. I rang up the club and you weren't there.

MARK. As a matter of fact I was delayed at the Foreign Office and at the last possible moment a long dispatch came in——

CAROLINE. Not one of those complicated cyphers——

MARK. Very complicated, my dear——

CAROLINE. From Mesopotamia? Of course, it couldn't be—it's called something else now, isn't it?

OSCAR. I'm sorry you had to throw stones at my window.

The trouble is, you can never hear the front door bell here—— (CAROLINE *is looking idly round the room.*)

CAROLINE (*looking at wireless*). Oh, so that's where the little wireless went to. I've always wondered.

MARK. I—er—lent it to Oscar—I'm sorry. I should have told you.

OSCAR. Yes. It's been astonishingly useful. Astonishingly —six o'clock news——

CAROLINE. At twenty to, exactly, Denis said I could ring him up. What's the time now? Oh, the clock from the morning room. Nearly twenty-five to. But that clock always gains about three minutes a week, dear. Do you regulate it?

MARK. Do you?

OSCAR. Oh yes, Constantly. Charming present of Mark's, wasn't it?

CAROLINE. We've got seven and a half minutes. Have you ordered a car, darling?

MARK. Yes.

CAROLINE. Well, we'll send it away. I've brought the Daimler.

MARK. Oh, you have, my dear. That's splendid. (*In a whisper to* OSCAR.) Doris, Doris.

OSCAR. Oh—Caroline—by the way—a friend of mine is coming with us——

CAROLINE. Oh, yes. The Minister for War?

MARK. No, no. He chucked, too.

CAROLINE. What a lot of chucking.

MARK. Well, as a matter of fact, it's a lady, a friend of Oscar's.

CAROLINE. Oh. Mabel Brightlingsea? Dear old Mabel. Is she quite up to going out these days?

OSCAR. No. As a matter of fact, Caroline, I don't think you know her. It's just a young friend of mine—I thought I'd give her a treat, you know. (*Crossing to champagne.*)

Well, now, Caroline, could I perhaps offer you a glass
of champagne? It's Moet and Chandon '37—— (*The
flat door slams.*) Here is the lady.

DORIS *enters.*

DORIS. Well, that's done. I hope I haven't made you late,
Major.

CAROLINE. Doris, isn't this nice. I'm coming to the first
night with you.

DORIS (*turning and seeing* CAROLINE). Oh!

CAROLINE. Yes, my temperature went down and I got up.
This is the dress you showed me at Fabia's. How do you
like it in white?

DORIS. Oh, it's lovely.

CAROLINE. Isn't it nice I am able to wear it for the first
night, after all. And I hear there's still a seat.

DORIS. Yes. Chloe's.

CAROLINE. Chloe?

DORIS. That's the tall girl I told you I thought the General
would like to meet, do you remember?

CAROLINE. Oh, yes.

DORIS. Well, she got taken quite queer—a bad oyster, it
was—and so it'll be just the four of us—which will be
ever so nice, won't it? And nice for Denis, too, having
his Mum and Dad out front after all.

CAROLINE. Are you ready to start, dear?

DORIS. No. I'll just fix my hair, won't be a tick. (*She goes
into the bedroom.*)

CAROLINE. What a sweet girl that is. So much nicer than
that horrid existentialist, in Paris.

MARK (*groaning*). Caroline! Caroline! Caroline!

CAROLINE. Yes, my dear?

MARK. You have shocked and blasted me to the very depths
of my being.

CAROLINE. Have I, my dear? I do apologise. I would have
avoided it if I possibly could—but after you went

G

blithering away on the telephone just now about: "I don't know where he is, milady"—darling, what a Cockney accent—really—I realised I'd have to take drastic action if I wanted to see Denis play Mark Antony tonight.

MARK. How long have you known, how long?

CAROLINE. Now, let me see. (*To* OSCAR.) When was it that Oscar first let his flat to a Mr Mark Wright. That's quite a long time ago now, isn't it, dear?

OSCAR. Thirty-three years ago, only thirty-three years.

CAROLINE. Is it really? How time flies, to be sure. Well, now, when bills started turning up on my desk for decorations to No. 12 Wilbraham Terrace——

MARK. Oh, my God!

CAROLINE. And letters addressed to Mr Mark Wright— darling, I do hope you're not as careless with confidential documents at the Embassy as you are with letters addressed to Mr Mark Wright.

MARK. I told you Mark Wright was an old friend of mine——

CAROLINE. You told me lots of things, dear, and you took the greatest trouble to make me believe them. If you tell lies to Foreign Ministers as clumsily as you tell them to me, I wonder that anyone ever speaks to us at the United Nations.

OSCAR. Oh, what a tangled web we weave——

CAROLINE. No, not a very tangled web, a remarkably simple web on the whole. And when—to crown it all, you go and choose a girl from a shop where I get my dresses and, of course, pick the very one whom I know particularly well——

MARK. Doris never, never mentioned a word.

CAROLINE. Of course not, dear. I swore her to utter secrecy—and she's a sweet girl, so I knew she would never give me away.

MARK. Caroline, for thirty-three years you have been deceiving me. You have just made the most immoral and unprincipled statement it has ever been my lot to listen to.

CAROLINE. Is it immoral and unprincipled? What do you think, Oscar?

OSCAR. I'm afraid, Caroline, that I must tell you that I am as deeply shocked as Mark.

CAROLINE. Oh, well, then perhaps I *am* unprincipled and immoral. You see, I've never been much tempted to the more conventional forms of immorality—though I admit—now I come to think of it—that on just a couple of occasions it might have been rather nice to have been Caroline Wright——

MARK (*aghast*). Oh—Caroline!

CAROLINE. But I never did, dear. I never did.

MARK. That, at least, is something.

CAROLINE (*brightly*). So as I've never been immoral in other ways, this immorality of mine in not ever having made an issue of Mr Mark Wright was really only, I suppose, what you might call—having my little fling.

MARK. Well, Oscar, I ask you——

CAROLINE. I nearly made an issue once, you know, over that first girl—that silly flapper—what was her name? Mark, what was her name? (MARK *doesn't reply*.) Oscar—that silly girl he met on a bus—Daphne Prentice, that was it. (MARK *groans*.).

CAROLINE. Yes. I nearly made an issue over her. But then I thought—well, if I do—he'll drop this silly girl all right, but he'll hate me for ever afterwards. So what's the use? And then there was that time when you were thinking of leaving the Diplomatic because of that creature—what was her name now—Nora Patterson— and what an issue I'd have made over that—but then suddenly you dropped the whole idea—and I breathed again——

MARK. Ah. Denis told you that, I suppose?

CAROLINE (*puzzled*). Denis? Mark—you don't mean it was Denis who got you to change your mind on that? Oh—I knew of course, you wouldn't have done it yourself—but I always imagined it was Oscar who rescued you. It was Denis, was it? (*Fondly.*) Oh, what a clever boy, and he never even told his mother!

MARK. This is my wife, Oscar. This is the woman I have always looked up to as a pillar of rectitude and simple-heartedness.

CAROLINE. Simple-heartedness doesn't mean half-wittedness, dear. Anyway I made no issue over Nora Patterson, because I didn't have to after all—and none of the myriad others have really bothered me——

MARK (*groaning*). What!

CAROLINE. You see from the beginning I thought to myself—well, this Mark Wright business must go rather deep. I'm his wife, and if he really wants to change his identity from time to time, then it must, in some way, be my fault. Something that I can't give him, that he wants and can find elsewhere. I would have liked to have been Mrs Mark Wright, but I knew I couldn't be. I knew I couldn't ever be anything more than the wife of Mark Binfield—and as I wanted, more than most things, to go on being that, I realised I had to give up all claims on Mark Wright. And I did. Except, of course, that I had to do my best to see that Mr Wright came to no harm. In Paris, for instance, we always have to have him followed by the Embassy detectives. (*To* OSCAR.) He will go to such dreadful dives in Montparnasse. (MARK *groans again and covers his face with his hands.* CAROLINE *looks at her watch.*) Right. Time to ring up Denis. Oscar, get the number, will you? It's Waterloo 6849.

OSCAR *goes to the telephone.*

CAROLINE. Darling, I am feeling so nervous for Denis tonight. How nice that you will be there to hold my hand. Darling, why will you wear stiff collars with your dinner jacket. It looks so old-fashioned. (MARK *groans for the last time.* CAROLINE *squeezes his hand.*)

OSCAR. Oh, stage door . . . would you put me through to Mr Wright . . . it's his mother . . .

CAROLINE *gets up and goes to the telephone.* OSCAR *comes to* MARK, *who is still sunk gloomily in his chair*

CAROLINE (*at telephone*). Denis? . . . Darling, just to wish you everything in the world . . . yes, I'm coming. No, I am much better . . .

OSCAR. The best of both worlds? How easy if you have the genius for it——

MARK. Oh, Oscar. The shame of it! The shame!

CAROLINE (*on telephone*). Oh, darling, how sweet of you. Yes, of course, we'd love it. (*To* MARK.) He's chucking his first night party and asking us to supper afterwards. Isn't that nice? (*Into telephone.*) Darling, how do you feel? (MARK *rises.*) Don't worry, you'll be splendid. Well, darling boy, everything in the world. Here's father. (*She hands the receiver to* MARK, *who takes it in a daze.*)

DORIS (*entering*). Is my hair all right?

MARK (*on telephone*). Denis? . . . Yes. Just to wish you the very best of luck, old chap . . . Well, as a matter of fact, I've just been saying to Oscar that I consider it the best Mark Antony I have seen . . . (*He catches* OSCAR's *eye*) since Tree . . .

OSCAR (*in a whisper*). Ask him about bloody.

MARK. Shut up. (*Into telephone.*) What, old chap . . . Mother? Yes, I knew you'd be glad . . .

OSCAR (*louder*). Ask him about bloody.

MARK. Go away. (*Into telephone.*) Oh, it's only your Uncle

Oscar. Some ridiculous idea he has that it's "bloody piece of earth," and not "bleeding . . ." (*To* OSCAR.) There you are, you see. You've gone and put him off. He says he can't remember himself now——

OSCAR. Oh, Lord. (*He snatches the receiver: frantically into telephone.*) Look, old chap. it doesn't matter, you know. Just say the first thing that comes into your head—bloody or bleeding—it doesn't matter, old chap. It really doesn't—— (MARK *snatches the receiver back.*)

MARK. Pay no attention to him, Denis. He's drunk . . . Well, won't keep you, old chap. All the very best——

DORIS. Give him mine, too——

MARK. Oh, and Doris sends her love, too . . . No, Denis, there's no point in lowering your voice and being tactful. I haven't made a bloomer . . . Yes, well it's a long story. I'll tell you later. (*He rings off.*)

CAROLINE. Come on, now. We're going to be late. Oscar, will you escort Doris to the car? Where's my bag?

DORIS. Come along, Major, you must look after me to-night.

OSCAR. That will be a pleasure, my dear.

DORIS. We might do a little dancing later.

DORIS *and* OSCAR *go out.*

CAROLINE (*running her finger on top of the radio*). Really. I must speak to Williams about the way he keeps this flat.

MARK (*hopelessly*). You must speak to Williams.

CAROLINE. I have a little confession to make about Williams, darling. With the servant problem so terrible, it did seem such a waste—so he does occasionally pop in to Belgrave Square, and help out. Just now and then, you know.

MARK. Just now and then?

CAROLINE. I knew you wouldn't mind.

MARK. You knew I wouldn't mind?

She inspects the bronze head of SYLVIA.

CAROLINE. What a very pretty face Sylvia did have. Do you know, dear, she still looks a little like that.

MARK. What?

CAROLINE. Of course, she's quite old now. What would she be exactly? A year younger than you, isn't she? Sixty-three. Yes. She looks all of sixty-three, I'm afraid.

MARK (*aghast*). You mean—you know her?

CAROLINE. Sylvia Willoughby-Grant? My dear, we play bridge together.

MARK (*laughing hysterically*). No. No—not that! No, Caroline—you can't pull that one on me. She's in South Africa——

CAROLINE. My dear, didn't you know? She came back years ago—before the war. She lives in Chester Square. I tell you what would be rather nice. I'll have her to dinner next week——

MARK. Oh, God!

CAROLINE. She really looks quite sweet, you know. It'll really be such fun for you to meet her again after all these years, won't it?

MARK. Caroline, you wicked, wicked woman. I give in. Unconditional surrender. Sylvia now goes the way of Mark Wright——

CAROLINE. Well, darling, in a way I suppose that's only just, isn't it—seeing that up to now it's been Mark Wright that's always gone the way of Sylvia. (OSCAR *comes back with his overcoat on, and carrying* MARK's.) All right, all right, Oscar, we're coming. Don't look so dejected, dear. You'll like her very much, I know, when you meet her. A very sweet and charming old lady. (*She smiles at him. After a pause he smiles back. She goes out.*)

OSCAR (*as he helps* MARK *on with his overcoat*). What does it feel like to grow from 17 to 64 in five minutes? Having your cake and eating it, eh? (*He chuckles.*)

MARK. Well—all I can say is this. I have jolly well had my cake and I have jolly well eaten it—and that's more than can jolly well be said for most people, including yourself, so yah!

OSCAR. A little prep school, wasn't it, for an ambassador?

MARK. That wasn't an ambassador speaking. That was the last recorded utterance of Mr Mark Wright. (*Looking round room.*) Pity. It was fun. Oh, well, never say die, I suppose. (*They move towards doors.* OSCAR *turns off lights.*) Come on, Oscar. (*They go out into the hall together.*)

CURTAIN